MW01702494

THE TALK!

FROM A BIBLICAL PERSPECTIVE

BY

Gayle L. Bucher

CPR
Creating Positive Relationships
Carmel, Indiana

Cartoons by
Brandon Corbin

Graphic Design by
Angel D. Bates

Copyright © 1997 by Gayle L. Bucher

Creating Positive Relationships
30 N. Rangeline Road, Suite A
Carmel, Indiana 46032
(317) 846-0386

All rights reserved.
Printed and bound in the United States of America

No part of this book may be reproduced in any form without permission in writing from the publisher, except in the case of worksheets or handouts as indicated.

ISBN: 0-9634373-7-2

Table of Contents

ACKNOWLEDGMENTS

I am extremely grateful to the many authors who have enlightened my thinking and presented practical ideas for parenting and communicating with young people about the complexity of sexuality. I would also like to give credit to the creative friends in my life who have shared their ideas to further develop CREATING POSITIVE RELATIONSHIPS and this book for parents. Special thanks to Bill Corbin, Lori Borgman Nye and Lisa Miller for their editing and encouragement. Much gratitude and love to my husband, Clint, and my two daughters, Rochelle and Jessica, for their patience and support during the writing of this book. Finally, I thank God for His inspiration and empowerment to complete this work.

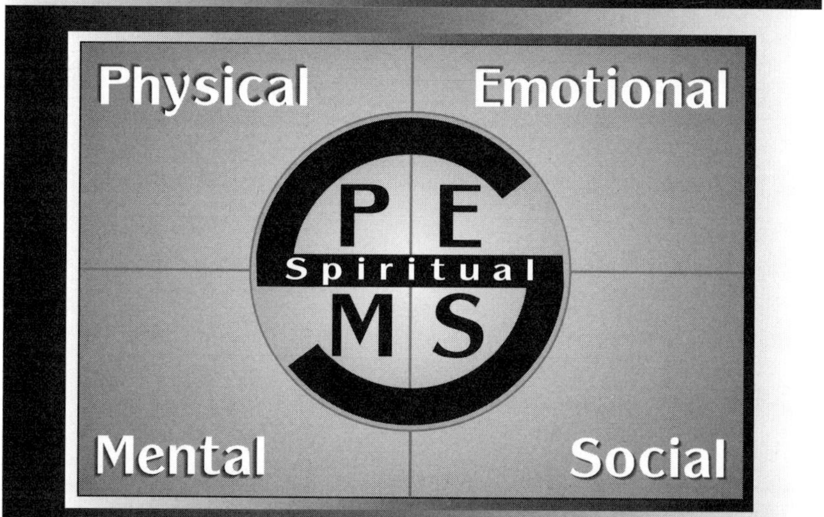

"It's not just a physical thing!"

Sexuality –
A Whole Person Issue

In 1986 I began working at a local crisis pregnancy center. The crisis phone line rang off the wall, particularly on weekends. I fielded many questions from anxious teenagers.

"I'm feeling nauseated and bloated. Does that mean that I'm pregnant?"

"Can I get pregnant when I'm having my period?"

"Can I get AIDS from playing around?"

"I had sex last night for the first time; how soon can I get a pregnancy test?"

"If I get an abortion, do my parents have to know about it?"

"Can my girlfriend get pregnant every day of the month?"

"If I take the 'morning after' pill, will it hurt me if I didn't need it?"

"Do I have any legal rights to stop my girlfriend from getting an abortion?"

The questions went on and on. Many young people I talked to were convinced that most dating relationships should include sex. Some girls I talked with felt obligated to have sex because their date took them to McDonald's or to a movie. Others were raped and believed they deserved it. Some teens had sex to prove their womanhood or manhood. Still others had sex to show their friends that they were not homosexual.

Working at the center, I soon learned that sexually transmitted diseases, unplanned pregnancy and broken hearts know no socioeconomic boundaries. I counseled with 11-year-old pregnant adolescents, 16-year-old preppie cheerleaders, inner-city single moms and hardened, drug-addicted runaways. They were all looking for the answers to the emptiness in their lives. They were looking for intimacy, acceptance and companionship.

They lacked information, but even more importantly, they lacked understanding. As I listened to their stories and shared their pain, I desperately wanted to help young people make wiser, healthier decisions. I wanted to reach them before they came through the doors of the crisis pregnancy center.

Most of our efforts to educate teens about sexuality had failed miserably. It was time to teach young people about the complexity of sexuality and to help them make decisions that would spare them from painful consequences. They needed a course that would teach them about the mental, emotional, social and spiritual aspects of sexuality, as well as the physical aspects.

After spending four years hearing too many sad stories and realizing that my clients were getting younger and younger, I decided it was time to develop a sexual education program that was factual, thought-provoking and life-changing. I researched existing curriculums and began to develop *CREATING POSITIVE RELATIONSHIPS.* My main objective was to provide public schools with a course that would teach a whole-person approach (addressing the physical, mental, emotional, social aspects of sexuality) and help students learn how to have healthy relationships. I also wanted to design a complementary course for parochial schools and youth groups that would address the spiritual aspects of sexuality. I called this program *CREATING POSITIVE RELATIONSHIPS PLUS.*

One of the first places I taught was at an alternative school for students who had been expelled from the regular classroom. They had gotten into all kinds of trouble; many were already mothers and fathers, and most were headed on a collision course with life. To my surprise, the students were attentive and asked many questions. They were amazed by the option of sexual abstinence and thoughtfully considered the material presented.

CREATING POSITIVE RELATIONSHIPS has been well received by public and private schools around the country. In 1990, the first year I began teaching the whole-person concept of sexuality, the program reached 700 students. By 1997, over 70,000 students had received the *CREATING POSITIVE RELATIONSHIPS* course in the Indianapolis area. In addition, programs were being taught in other parts of Indiana, various other states and internationally in Russia. Each year, schools continue to extol the value and practicality of this course.

Young people want to understand themselves better and to enjoy their lives. I am convinced that many parents want to impart helpful information to their children. Yet, as the parent of two daughters, I also know how awkward and difficult this task can be.

Society generates a lot of confusing messages about sexuality today, not only for children, but for parents as well: *When should we start teaching about sex? How much should we explain? Should we teach about birth control and protection from diseases? Is it realistic to expect our teens to abstain?*

Most parents would like for their children to postpone sexual activity until marriage because we are aware of the serious health ramifications of sex outside of a mutually faithful, monogamous relationship. In addition, Christian parents realize the spiritual consequences of premarital sex and the devastation of a disobedient life. If you are a parent who has been looking for a resource to guide you in presenting information about the physical, mental, emotional, social and spiritual benefits of sexual abstinence, this book is for you. This book is designed to help parents teach their children about sexuality and communicate their values in a relaxed, nonthreatening way.

Throughout this book, I have developed the whole-person concept of sexuality. Sexuality affects every aspect of ourselves—physical, mental, emotional, social and spiritual. "Having sex" is far more than just a physical act with physical consequences.

The physical aspect referred to in this book relates to our physical bodies. This includes the needs of our physical bodies, as well as the physical health of our bodies. The mental aspect refers to our thought processes and our perceptions about ourselves, others and life. The emotional aspect encompasses our feelings and our senses. The social aspect addresses our personal relationships. Our spirituality includes our personal belief system which provides a framework for our moral values and our perspective on life. This book is written from a Christian perspective, with the *Bible* as the ultimate authority. I have shared some selected scriptures that apply to this topic. At times, I have found that *The MESSAGE* paraphrase by Eugene H. Peterson[1] helps teens to get a better grasp on what the *Bible* teaches. I have quoted some of this paraphrase that I have found to be helpful. You may find a number of other scriptures that you would like to use. Be careful not to use the *Bible* as a 2x4 over the head. That approach will not endear the Word of God to your child. As the Spirit leads you, gently weave scripture into your teaching and conversation.

In order to meet the needs of a variety of parents, I have included some basic factual information, along with insights from my work with teenagers and my role as a parent. Depending on where you are in the process of parenting, some parts of the book may be more applicable to you than others. Because we interact with our children daily, sharing these concepts obviously will be an ongoing process, rather than a one time talk.

The following is a brief explanation of the basic flow of this book:

Chapter 1 begins with some pointers on how to open communication with your children. It explains where to begin your discussion and how to use a creative demonstration to set the stage. Set aside a special time that is free of distractions. You may want to plan a weekend retreat by yourselves or include some other parents and their children who have the same agenda. Mix the weekend with talks and fun together. I did this with my daughters and some of our mutual friends. It turned out quite well. Planning a weekend together communicates that your child is very valuable to you and the topic of sexuality is approachable and important. Know your children and the type of setting in which they will feel the least amount of self-consciousness. Don't expect them to be thrilled with the idea at any time. That's okay. Forge ahead.

Chapter 2 covers the whole-person needs that often motivate sexual behaviors. We all have physical, mental, emotional, social and spiritual needs that are a part of who we are as a person. We have perceptions or thoughts about how we can get those needs met. We begin to take action or behave in a certain way to try to meet our needs. This behavior will result in positive or negative consequences, depending on the behavior that we choose. Numerous studies have asked teens why they became involved sexually before marriage. Their reasons are all related to their whole-person needs.

Chapter 3 explains the whole-person consequences to sexual activity outside of a marriage relationship. Information concerning pregnancy, sexually transmitted diseases, along with other less visible consequences are explored. If you or your child are not thoroughly convinced that abstinence until marriage is the best choice, consider covering this chapter first. I have found young people much more receptive to postponing sexual involvement when they are first taught about the painful consequences of teenage sex.

Chapters 4 and **5** explore the process and the many benefits of whole-person maturity (growing up in every aspect of our lives). Growing up is a lifetime process. Physical maturity is automatic if we are reasonably healthy. Mental, emotional, social and spiritual maturity all take a great deal of effort. Our efforts to develop whole-person maturity encourage behaviors and choices that result in many benefits for our lives. Because this is a lifetime process, we all (parents included) are in need of continual encouragement towards maturity. Touting the benefits of mature decision-making helps teens to understand that they can actually have some control over their future. Since this is a time when they are lobbying for more control in their lives, this message begins to appeal to them. They can make choices, but they are also responsible for their choices and the corresponding consequences. Show them the correlation between responsibility and freedom. The more responsible they become, the more freedoms they'll enjoy (age appropriate, of course). An enthusiastic comparison between the many benefits of sexual abstinence and the hefty consequences of sexual activity provides a solid foundation on which to rest your case.

Chapter 6 addresses the topics of love, dating and commitment in relationships. This includes the confusion about love and sex, the media sex blitz, dating ideas and practical ways to maintain a goal of abstinence. Also included are helpful suggestions for the teen who has been sexually active and desires to change.

Chapter 7 takes a brief look at the difficult topics of homosexuality, masturbation and sexual abuse.

I have also included an Appendix which gives factual information to help you answer questions your child may ask. You may want to keep a good dictionary handy as well.

Special features throughout the book are included to help you with ***THE TALK!*** **Let's Talk About It** and **Let's Take A Closer Look** allow you to open communication and make a practical application with your teen about the topic being addressed. **Let's Think About It** gives you a little phrase that sums up an important point. You might want to post these sayings on the refrigerator or a message board for an occasional reminder. **Scriptures to Consider** offers Biblical references for you to examine which will help your discussions stay God-centered. **Creative Demonstrations** are great visuals to help teens remember the important concepts that are being taught. These demonstrations are also very effective with groups of teens.

This book can be used in a variety of ways. If the whole-person concept of sexuality is unfamiliar to you, it may be helpful to read the book through thoroughly before you try to communicate the lessons to your children. Even if this is not a new concept, give the book a quick run-through before you begin and highlight the points you want to stress. Some parents may want to go through the book methodically with their teens. Others may want to pick out the parts they want to emphasize and use them at opportune moments. The more familiar you become with the concepts, the more natural you will feel in sharing them with your child. You also will be preparing yourself for those openings for conversation that occur at the most unlikely times. If you plan to use the demos, practice them a few times before you present them and take note of the suggested points to make.

Most importantly, be yourself. Take the material and communicate it in the way that feels natural for you. My sincere desire is that you will be given information and helpful ideas to expound on ***THE TALK!*** with your child. Go for it!

Chapter 1

"We can't put this off forever!"

Getting Ready

Prepare yourself... We all have perceptions about sexuality that are based upon our own experiences. Think ahead of time about any areas where you may find it difficult to be objective because of painful memories or mistakes you made. Be honest with yourself and your child when you approach these topics. Pray that God will guide you and help you to effectively communicate with your child.

Set the stage... Since sex is a topic that can elicit anything from embarrassment to shear panic, deciding where to have these talks is crucial. Choose the most comfortable room in the house that affords some privacy if others will be going in and out. Weather permitting, pick a relaxing spot outside. Keep some snacks handy to ease the tension. How many talks will it take? That is up to you and your child. Start with meeting once a week at the same time and take as long as you need or do a retreat weekend. If your relationship with your child is less than friendly, you may want to read this book, note the important points and spoon feed them at opportune moments. Our second daughter would put her hands over her ears when she wasn't going to listen anymore. That was a pretty good signal that I was laying it on a little too heavy. Don't preach or lecture. Watch for their body language to tell you when their mind is full and take a break. Trudging through the material just to get it over with will defeat the purpose of ***THE TALK!***

Set the tone... Young people appreciate being treated like adults. Try to step out of your parenting role (no small task) and talk with your child as if you were talking to a close friend. Share some funny stories about some of your experiences growing up and how you learned about sex. Think about what *you* wanted to know but were afraid to ask. Our children need to know that we want to help them sort through this complex issue.

Studies continue to confirm that the more openly parents discuss their sex-related values and beliefs with teens, the less their children display negative sexual attitudes or promiscuous sexual behavior. Children also want to hear about sex from their parents before they get lessons at school—this helps them to feel less ignorant. Sex education should begin with biological facts but must include moral values and character education. That is why it should be the primary responsibility of the parent.

Where do you begin? Hopefully, you have laid the groundwork for your adolescent/teen discussions with age-appropriate talks as your child has been in the process of growing up. The best way to give your child sex education is by taking advantage of teaching opportunities when they happen (bath tub, new babies, pets giving birth, inappropriate behavior observed). Teach your children about modesty and the appropriate places and times to talk about sex. Explain good touch, bad touch.

Children need to know the basic facts before puberty. Puberty is occurring earlier than in the past, dropping from 16.5 years in 1870 to 12.5 years today.[2] In my opinion, nine or ten years old is an appropriate age to begin explaining the facts about sexuality. Before that age, answer any questions they have without getting too explicit. Often, parents misread the sex-related questions of the younger child and dump the whole truckload of information on them.

For example, have you heard the story about the child who asks: "Mom, what is sex?" She gets all flustered and blurts out the facts of life to him. He responds with: "If you know so much about sex, how come you got an 'F' in it?" She gives him a bewildered look. He continues with:

"I was looking at your driver's license and it said that you got an 'F' in sex?"

Watch out for those innocent questions—perhaps getting clarification of what they are asking before you give a response is a wise suggestion. There are numerous books available to help you give that first sex talk. You may want to read a book together to break the ice. If you have neglected to do this, it is never too late to start. Review the basic anatomy and development information in the APPENDIX on pages 166-171. Most likely, by fifth grade, your child will have received this instruction in school. If you're nervous, focus more on the subject than on your insecurities.

One reason parents are so reluctant to talk about sexual issues with their children is because they have regrets about their sexual history. *"How can I promote premarital abstinence when I didn't abstain?"* Be prepared that your child will most likely ask you if you abstained. You can be truthful without being explicit. Be willing to admit your mistakes and share some of the consequences of your mistakes. Parents who are willing to admit their mistakes to their children model the importance of integrity and vulnerability. Your child will be more likely to be truthful and to admit bad choices to you if you don't portray yourself as perfect by denying your shortcomings.

Divorced parents sometimes have an additional challenge if their "ex" is not modeling or promoting the same character values and abstinence standards they are teaching their child. If there is open communication between parents, try to explain the importance of supporting each other in this area. Unfortunately, it is difficult to control what your child may experience when in the care of another person. The best that you can hope for is that your children will respect your wishes as they realize your love for them. Bad-mouthing your ex usually backfires. If you suspect that your child is being exposed to pornography or sexual harassment, seek legal counsel.

Before you embark on the mission of teaching your child about sexuality, review the following:

POINTERS FOR *THE TALK!*

- *Emphasize that sex is a beautiful gift from God that is worth respecting and protecting.*
- *Sex is good and wonderful in the right context (not dirty or shameful). God's standard of sex only in marriage is designed to protect us from painful consequences and to provide His best for our lives.*
- *Be honest when you don't know the answers. Seek counsel and read books for information.*
- *Repeat important concepts often, as well as any information that may initially go over their heads because of embarrassment.*
- *Keep your sense of humor. This is a heavy subject that requires some lightheartedness!*
- *Stress the positive benefits of waiting just as much as you caution about negative consequences.*

- *Role-play potential situations to help your children prepare ahead of time.*
- *Watch your reactions to their questions and comments. Don't gasp, even if you're shocked. If they sense that you can't handle what they're saying, they will stop talking to you.*
- *Maintain confidentiality. If your children learn you've been sharing their comments with your friends, they will feel betrayed.*
- *When your children seem troubled, don't interrogate. Open communication with comments like "You seem to be upset..."*
- *Be patient—withdrawal can be a defense mechanism but may be just normal adolescent behavior.*

IN ADDITION

- *Let your children know how much you love them and that they are priceless to you.*
- *Consciously model the character traits in your own life that you are striving to teach your children. Admit and apologize for your mistakes.*
- *Be actively involved in your children's school and aware of the sex education that is taught. Offer positive alternatives to your school if they do not have a strong abstinence program that includes character education.*
- *Seek out churches, synagogues, organizations or clubs that promote your values to strengthen the abstinence message you are teaching at home.*
- *Pray often for guidance and protection for your children.*

According to teen surveys, the following are common reasons why teens find it difficult to talk to or listen to their parents. Perhaps becoming aware of what teens indicate create barriers in communication will help you to avoid the common pitfalls of communication breakdown with your teen.

WHY TEENS DON'T TALK TO THEIR PARENTS

- Parents are poor listeners and are often preoccupied with other things. They are halfway listening while they are thinking of a response. Sometimes they lose track of what is being said. Often they are restless and impatient.
- The family is so independent that they do not share what is going on in each other's lives.
- Parents are so busy; they are only available to get the basic facts about where the children are going, what they are doing etc. and to give their instructions.
- Parents tend to interrupt their teens and finish their sentences. They make quick judgments and react to what they think they are hearing before they listen to the whole story.
- The family is stressed. The relationship between the parent and teen is a silent war because of unresolved conflict.

WHY TEENS DON'T LISTEN TO THEIR PARENTS

- Teens won't listen when they sense the parent is a hypocrite (doesn't walk the talk).

- Teens sense when a parent is not firm in his own convictions, so they lack respect for the parent.
- Parents use put downs or sarcasm to make their points. Teens lose confidence in their parents' sincerity and think any of the parents' positive comments are controlling and manipulative.
- Parents become too controlling, not allowing the teen to develop independence with responsibility.
- Teens tune out a parent when the parent nags or preaches at them.

Teens often are reluctant to talk with their parents about sexual issues. Don't let their reluctance keep you from this important responsibility. Maybe they would feel more comfortable if you included several of their friends and made it a group discussion. (Get permission from the other parents.) The creative demonstrations work very well with groups of teens.

IN SUMMARY

Before you begin this adventurous and courageous journey to communicate with your child about sexual issues, take a good look at yourself. What psychological and emotional baggage will you be bringing along with you? Be prepared to be honest with your child about your own insecurities and your mistakes. Don't be afraid to admit things that you do not know. Some of their questions may be related to the mass media exposure of sexual issues. You have gotten along in life just fine without knowing about every sexual term or act. Answer their questions when you can and offer to find the answers to those that are important to know. Make every effort to keep the atmosphere of ***THE TALK!*** relaxed and low key. Keep your sense of humor. Practice being a good listener every day. Your children will be more open to listening to your counsel if they feel they are being heard. Pray earnestly that God will help you to communicate the truth with love. We cannot afford to dodge this responsibility or let others be their primary sex educator.

REMEMBER:

We are ***RESPONSIBLE TO — love, teach and discipline our children.***

We are NOT ***RESPONSIBLE FOR — their decisions and their choices.***

Allow your children to suffer the consequences of their wrong choices when they are young. This helps to teach them that they are responsible for their choices. Do not beat yourself up if you have done your best to teach your children, to impart your family values, and they have made choices contrary to your instruction. They may have to live with some painful consequences and they will need your loving support. Do not blame yourself for their choices.

You may want to open ***THE TALK!*** with the following demonstration.

CREATIVE DEMONSTRATION

Make the following points with this demonstration:

- *Our sexuality is a valuable gift from God.*
- *If we do not place value on our sexuality, it will be misused and abused.*
- *Saving our gift shows our future marriage partner how much we care about him/her.*
- *Consequences of premarital sex will go with us into a marriage.*

Gift-wrap a box and put a tie (for a boy) or a handkerchief (for a girl) inside the box. Explain to your teen that sexuality is a precious gift from God. *What happens to the value of your gift if it is unwrapped and used before the appropriate time (marriage)?* Describe a situation where a teen does not put high value on the gift of sexuality. Open the box, take out the gift, crumple it, pretend to soil it (pizza on the tie, blow your nose in the handkerchief) to indicate the teen giving the gift prematurely and someone using/abusing it. When the relationship breaks up, the teen tries to wrap the gift again and make it appear to be unused. You might repeat this scenario several times.

What happens to the value of the gift? Who wants to receive a used gift? Would you like to receive a used gift?

[Your dating partner will attach the same value to your sexuality that you attach to it.]

Do you plan to be faithful to your future marriage partner?
[Most likely, your marriage partner is alive today. Saving your gift of sexuality shows that you saved yourself as the ultimate love commitment to your future spouse. Your faithfulness should begin today. If not, your former sexual experiences will be taken with you into your marriage relationship.]

If you want to have a lively discussion, substitute underwear for the tie and handkerchief. *Would your teen want to wear someone's used underwear?* (Gross!) Explain that the more intimate or close contact something (like underwear) or someone has with us (like sexual intercourse), the more special it *should* be to us.

Note: For teens who have already lost their virginity and would like to make a new beginning, encourage them that this **is** *possible. When they reassign high value to their sexuality, their gift will regain its value.*

Scriptures to Consider

Proverbs 3:6, II Corinthians 5:17, II Corinthians 7:10-11, I John 1:9

Let's Think About It...

"Put a MARRIAGE price tag on your gift of sexuality — don't settle for less."

Chapter 2

"Who needs it?!"

Whole-Person Needs

In the beginning of creation, God had a perfect relationship with mankind. All of their needs were met in relationship with Him. When Adam and Eve chose to disobey God, they created a sin barrier (a dark void) between themselves and God. They succumbed to Satan's temptation to take charge of their world and reach for personal significance apart from God. Through the ages mankind has searched to fill this void with pleasures, things, people or mini gods. These efforts are futile—we must take our deepest needs for intimacy to Him. Our lives and relationships will be more fulfilling when we begin to understand this truth. The sacrifice of Jesus Christ made it possible for our relationship to be restored with God, so that once again we could have all of our needs met in Him (Philippians 4:19). Because of the Fall, each one of us is born with whole-person needs. These needs are normal and healthy. Our needs motivate behavior and our behavior produces consequences. Using sexual behavior to meet whole-person needs will result in painful whole-person consequences. This is why it is important to begin to understand the needs that can motivate sexual behavior and explore healthier ways to have those needs met. While working with teenagers at a crisis pregnancy center, I soon realized that young people were becoming sexually active for a variety of reasons, many of which were related to their needs as human beings.

WHY SOME TEENS BECOME INVOLVED SEXUALLY

- Trying to cure loneliness or unhappiness.
- Hoping to become more popular.
- Using physical sex to avoid having a close, caring relationship. (One partner is afraid of allowing the other to really know him/her).
- Satisfying curiosity from watching sex on TV, movies, or seeing in magazines and books.
- Proving their independence, especially to parents or God with whom they are angry.
- Thinking that if they have a baby, the baby will love them. (A baby is not capable of returning the love a young girl is needing.)

- Hoping they will be treated as an adult if they have a baby or a baby will keep their relationship together.
- Mistaking loving words and close feelings for love. They are looking for intimacy that sexual involvement can temporarily satisfy.
- Looking for approval from the opposite or the same sex when parental or family relationships are dysfunctional.
- Desiring the respect and approval of their friends while being challenged to prove their sexual prowess.

PHYSICAL NEEDS

Everyone has a basic human need for physical touch. Physical touch is pleasurable and desirable. Studies have shown that babies that are not held, caressed and given an ample amount of physical touch become unhealthy. Young people who are being denied the pleasure of appropriate physical touch in their families will seek to have that need met by others. Often, sexual promiscuity is the result of the deprivation of physical touch. At other times, it is the result of the crossing of appropriate boundaries of physical touch, as in sexual abuse. The victim of sexual abuse may erroneously begin to believe that their primary value rests in giving sexual pleasure to others. The basic need for physical touch can propel a teenager into promiscuity if their needs are not being met in healthy, appropriate ways. A hand on the shoulder, a hug or even a shoulder massage can help meet your teenager's need for physical touch.

Our bodies respond to physical touch and more intimate touch escalates our desire for sexual expression. Our sexual drives are very powerful. A comparison can be made between controlling our sexual drives and controlling the car we are driving. A car will soon careen out of control if we do not use the steering wheel and the brakes to guide it. Sexual drives will also careen out of control if we have not set guidelines and learned where to apply the brakes. Setting limits of physical affection in a premarital relationship helps us to exercise self-control. Setting limits of affection is a part of whole-person maturity which is discussed in Chapter 4, pages 92-96.

Our children need to know the basic facts about their bodies and how they function. When they reach adolescence, they are experiencing changes in their bodies and new sexual feelings. It is important for them to understand that these changes and feelings are normal. Often, curiosity leads the adolescent to begin to experiment with sexual activity. As a parent, you have the opportunity to teach them the facts about their bodies and to answer their questions. Both you and your children may feel uncomfortable discussing sex, but it is your responsibility as their parent to teach them about their bodies. They may tell you that they already know the facts, but this is often a ploy to avoid the discussion. Take a deep breath... you *can* do it and you *must* do it for their sakes. When you carefully explain the facts and answer their questions, you are removing some of the curiosity about sex that can motivate sexual experimentation. Refer to the ***APPENDIX*** on pages 166-176 for some basic anatomy information, fetal development facts, terms and diagrams to help with your discussion if needed.

We have our work cut out for us. We are living in a society that revolves around sex and feeds on the natural curiosity of our adolescents and teenagers. The primary message of the media today reflects an attitude of pursuing personal immediate gratification with little or no consequences. The subtle message that is woven through television, movies, books, magazines and music is to live for today. It's okay. Everybody does it. Teens are encouraged to show responsibility by using birth control and protection. Don't underestimate the influence of the media upon your child. Teens naturally have an attitude of indestructibility, and unfortunately, our media today encourages them to walk the path of destruction. Chapter 6 takes a closer look at the impact of the media on our minds and offers some assignments to teach your teen how to look for media brainwashing.

Let's Take a Closer Look...

Read the following situation to your child and discuss the questions to illustrate how the need for physical touch, curiosity and the effect of media can lead to sexual experimentation.

Jeff's family structure is a model of independence. Each member independently manages his own affairs with little consideration or consultation with the other family members. His dad and mom work lots of hours to provide for their family's needs. The children have always been encouraged to keep busy in lots of activities. Home seems to be just a place to sleep, eat and get moving again. There's very little conversation or interaction between the parents and the children. Jeff doesn't have any adult to talk to about what's going on in his life. He feels very alone in his family environment and has been spending more and more time with a new girlfriend. He also has been hanging out at his friend's house after school. They have been watching some sexually explicit movies and occasionally they explore the computer for sexual topics and pictures. Lately, Jeff has begun to pressure his girlfriend for more physical affection and they are moving toward sexual involvement at a rapid pace.

What are the factors that may be contributing to Jeff pressuring his girlfriend for more physical affection and eventually sex?
[Jeff's lack of attention and physical affection at home, his curiosity, media stimulation]

What can Jeff do to help himself resist the temptation to experiment with premarital sex?
[Talk to his parents about his needs—if they don't respond, seek healthy companionship through a club, team or youth group; stop stimulating his mind with sexual media; talk with a parent or trusted adult friend about his curiosity; ask questions and make himself

accountable to someone; find some new friends; set limits of physical affection with his girlfriend, ask God for the strength to overcome these temptations]

Let's Think About It...

"Our mind is our most important 'sexual organ'."

Filling our minds with sexual media stimulates our hormones and our desire for physical intimacy.

Scriptures to Consider

I Corinthians 10:13, Galatians 5:16-17, Philippians 4:8

MENTAL NEEDS

Our self-image is how we see ourselves. What we believe others think about us is very important to us. This basic need for acceptance and approval often motivates us to behave in ways that are unhealthy. We want to be respected and to have others recognize that we are competent to handle our lives. We want to gain knowledge, to understand life and to reach our goals for our lives.

Our teens need to feel valued by their parents. They may act like they don't care what we think of them, but they desperately need our parental affirmation. Above all, they need to understand how priceless they are to God. God asked His only Son to lay down His life for them, even before they were born and while they were still sinners. Christ freely gave His life and paid the ultimate cost so that their relationship with God could be restored. His sacrifice was not conditional—that we obey Him before He would love us. We love him because He loved us first! That's a phenomenal indication of our value to God—every single one of us! I think this is a great mystery to us because none of us can fathom sacrificing our life for one rebellious sinner. Beginning to understand this truth is a strong foundation for a healthy self-worth.

Scriptures to Consider

Romans 5:6-8, I John 4:19

CREATIVE DEMONSTRATION

Make the following points with this demonstration:

- We have value because we are God's creation.
- God has confirmed our value by giving His Son to save us.
- It's essential to believe what God says about us to battle against Satan's lies.

Use a paper plate and a china plate to illustrate what makes something valuable. Hold the plates and ask the following questions:

Which plate is more valuable and why?
[china—it may have a famous manufacturer, it's more durable, more expensive, not throwaway, may have sentimental value]

Several of the factors that give something value are:

A. **Who made it.**
B. **How it's made.**
C. **A personal value attached to it. (Something** *may be personally valuable to you that would have little or no value to someone else—a ring, a pillow, a stuffed animal etc.)*

How could we apply this to ourselves? Do we have value?

Who made us?
[Genesis 1:26]

How were we made?
[Psalm 139:14]

We are like a fine piece of china or artwork, beautifully, wonderfully crafted to be valued and enjoyed. We are not like a paper plate, designed to be used and then tossed aside. (Toss the plate for effect.)

How did God ultimately show us that He attaches great value to us?
[John 3:16]

Why is it important that we attach value to ourselves?
[God has clearly shown us how valuable we are to Him. Not appreciating our value is an insult to God.]

Sometimes we are not happy with the way God designed us. We think that we are too short, too tall, too skinny or too fat. We don't like ourselves. This hurts our Designer - God. He put all of Himself into us. We are made in His image - with a mind, feelings, a free will and a soul. When we struggle with our self-worth, we need to stop and ask ourselves, "Are we basing our self-worth on what God's Word says is true or are we basing it on what the world says is true?" When we begin to understand our value in God's sight, we will be thankful for the body He gave us and remember that our bodies are His temple (where He lives if we are a Christian). By His power, we will be able to ignore the lies of the world and treat our bodies with their God-given dignity.

Developing a strong sense of self-respect is essential in order to gain the respect and approval of others. *To respect means to show honor, to esteem or to show high regard.* If we see ourselves as people who are worthy of respect, we will not easily compromise our thoughts, our values and our goals to win the acceptance and approval of others. We will treat our bodies with high regard and not allow others to use or abuse us for their personal gratification.

Teaching our children that they are worthy of respect begins with our every day attitude towards them. Do we give them as much honor as we would a guest in our home? We are the authority figure in our child's life, but often we become power oriented and mutual respect gets lost in the struggle. How can our child respect us when we are acting like a power hungry adolescent? It's easy to get caught in power struggles when our teen is trying to gain some independence. Sometimes we have to remind ourselves that we are the adult and must maintain an attitude of respect—especially when our teenager has become most obnoxious. Our teens will test us to see whether we love them unconditionally. Only God can give us the power to love them when their behavior is unlovable. At the same time, we must insist that our children show us appropriate respect. They should be allowed to express their feelings, even when they are angry, as long as they verbalize themselves in a respectful manner. If they cannot control themselves, they should go somewhere to cool off before they can be heard. Do not put up with verbal abuse or disrespectful behavior. If you begin this training early, it will be easier to enforce this family rule when your children reach adolescence.

Another way to teach our children that they are worthy of respect is to show them that their feelings and opinions are valued by us. Occasionally asking teens for their opinion about a situation allows them to feel that their opinions are worthwhile. Of course, never put your child in the position of becoming your confidante or counselor. There will be many times when you and your teen will have different opinions and feelings about a multitude of issues. Teens are in the process of developing autonomy and often will take an opposing position so they can feel like their own person. Don't become too alarmed at some of their opinions. At this time of their lives, they can develop some pretty wild ideas. They'll figure it all out over time. Be careful that you don't insist that when there is a difference of opinion, you are always right and they are wrong. Agree to disagree, but you are in charge of the final decision as long as they are living with you. This reiterates to them that their feelings and opinions are valued.

As our children learn to respect themselves, they will be able to handle the pressures that challenge their values, desires and goals. They will not easily succumb to these pressures to gain the acceptance and approval of others. It is essential that they learn to value themselves and to respect others. Remind them that every person is created in the image of God and is worthy of respect. When we are disrespectful to God's creation, we are disrespectful to God.

Let's Think About It...

"No one will respect you, if you don't respect yourself."

Sometimes adolescents and teens will become sexually involved because they are trying to meet their need for acceptance, approval or respect. A healthy self-image greatly increases your child's ability to resist negative peer pressure. At other times, the motivation for sexual behavior may be to show their competence to make their own decisions and to become independent from parents or even God. This can be rebellious in nature. Explain to your teen that sexual involvement does not prove their competence as a man or a woman. Animals have sex. Does that make them more manly or womanly?

Let's Take A Closer Look...

Use the following examples according to the appropriate age level of your child. Discuss the questions to illustrate how the need for the respect and approval of others, proving one's competence or rebellion can lead to the compromise of one's values and sexual involvement.

Ryan got a note from his friend, Peter. It said, "Hey, Ryan, I heard you and Michelle are going out! I can't believe you haven't kissed her yet! What's your problem? You gay or something?"

Some of Jerry's friends have been teasing him because he's still a virgin. He's not all that interested in getting involved with a girl, but he's really getting tired of their harassment. He finally asked a girl out this weekend who has a reputation for being easy. He has to lose his virginity sometime; he might as well get it over with!

Jenny feels like her parents are nagging her all the time. They have too many rules and are always asking too many questions. Her mother is always telling her to be careful and it makes her feel like a baby. She thinks she's old enough to run her own life; in fact, she's having sex with her boyfriend and they'd ground her forever if they knew!

Why might Ryan, Jerry and Jenny get involved in certain behaviors even though they are not really ready?
[need for acceptance, approval, respect, competence with peers or parents, rebellion]

What are other ways of gaining respect, approval and competence without giving in to negative peer pressure or rebellion?
[develop talents and get help to gain more self-respect; find some new friends who have similar values; get family counseling to work out reasonable rules with parents if needed; learn about God's perspective on ourselves through *Bible* study and discussion]

HOW TO ENCOURAGE STRONG SELF-WORTH

Society stresses that the most important things in life that make us a worthy person are the **"3 B's"**

BODY — BUCKS/$ — BRAINS!

If we measure our self-worth by this criteria, we will experience a continual struggle. We will fail to measure up in one area or another.

BODY

Take a look around you and observe all of the messages that bombard us daily with the importance of how good-looking or shapely we are. These messages are difficult for all of us to ignore. Billions of dollars are spent trying to make ourselves look like the fashion model or the jock and to pursue the proverbial fountain of youth. At some point in our lives, (the sooner, the better) we must begin to accept ourselves and our bodies. It's important to stay in shape and take care of our bodies for good health, and we'll feel better about ourselves in the process. However, even the best jocks or loveliest models have something about their bodies they would change if they could. As parents, give specific, sincere compliments to your children about their physical attributes—not flattery—they know the difference!

It's no small feat to try to counter the perfect body image with the thought that character is far more important than the outside of the package.

Nevertheless, that is precisely what we must do. Here's another tough job—we must *believe it* and *practice it* ourselves.

How is this accomplished? Every day, turn on your radar for signs of good character development. Give your children affirmation when you observe qualities like showing respect, sensitivity, honesty, goodness, self-control, compromise, compassion and the like. Your children will begin to get the message that their character is what is most important—not how they look. This doesn't mean we should forego braces when "Johnnie's" teeth are going ten different directions or ignore "Suzi's" need for Retin-A for her complexion.

BUCKS $

The media suggests that when our life is over *"THE ONE WITH THE MOST TOYS WINS!"* Right? *I don't think so.* We all enjoy nice things—there's nothing wrong with that. However, when those things or lack of things are the measuring stick of our personal value, we're in big trouble. The most difficult part about parenting is that children model our attitude about life, more than what we tell them to do. Here's another character check for us. How important are the *bucks* and *things* to us? If we take a moment and look at the richest people in this world, often we see that their personal lives are a mess. Are they really happy? Probably not—especially if their self-worth depends on their financial success. Once again, balance is the key. When the current *hot* fashion item seems to be a necessity for your teen to show off at school, try implementing a clothing budget. If Johnnie or Suzi wants to use his/her hard earned bucks to cover the excess in the price, that's okay. Clothing budgets can ease the name brand clothing battle at any age. Teaching our children fiscal responsibility is one of our duties as parents. Teaching them about the importance of *things* will be manifested in our own attitudes toward money and materialism.

BRAINS

The importance of our intellectual ability and how it affects our self-worth may depend somewhat on our stage of life. If we're too smart in middle or high school, we may be labeled as a *nerd.* At most other times in our lives, intelligence is a desired and a most respected attribute. It becomes easy to base our self-image on our superb intelligence. This way of thinking can spell trouble because there are circumstances, such as health problems or accidents, that can alter our intellectual ability. If our intelligence or abilities have been the basis of our self-worth, we will find ourselves emotionally devastated. Since intelligence is primarily a gift at birth, at times we must learn to accept our limitations. It's been said that we use only a very small portion of our brains—so there is always room for improvement and growth. For those who are mentally handicapped, our attitude toward their personal worth makes a powerful statement regarding our appreciation of human life in general. Treating the handicapped with dignity and respect will go a long way to promote their personal self-worth.

It goes without saying that we should do everything within our power to help our children to be successful in education and in life-skills, keeping in mind their natural talents and abilities. Encourage them to build on their strengths. Sometimes it's a difficult balancing act to determine if they are working up to their ability or if their behavior is lazy and irresponsible. Be careful when they are in need of correction to point out their unacceptable behavior and not to attack their character. For example, it's better to say: *"Your behavior is lazy and irresponsible."* Don't say: *"You are lazy and irresponsible!"* Attacking character undermines self-worth. It's important to encourage intellectual and skill development, while at the same time keeping character development as a primary goal. Children need to know that it is not what they do that gives them value, but their character within.

CREATIVE DEMONSTRATION

Make the following points with this demonstration:

- Each person is unique and has value.
- It's what is inside that counts.
- Helping others and using our talents boost self-worth.
- Healthy self-esteem eliminates the emotional need to prove oneself through sexual activity.

Use two apples, one pretty and one bruised, to illustrate that it is what's on the *inside* that is important. Ask your child the following questions:

How are people like apples?
[skin, seeds, different shapes, colors, sizes etc.]

What qualities do you look for if you want to buy an apple?
[pretty, firm, no bruises, etc.]

Is it possible that an apple that looks wonderful on the outside can be rotten on the inside?
[yes, especially if it's covered with caramel or taffy]

Can that also be true with people?
[yes]

What's more important, how we look on the outside or who we are on the inside?
[inside]

I Samuel 16:7 tells us what is important to God. It says that man looks at the outer appearance, but God looks at the heart. Jesus reprimanded the Pharisees in Matthew 23 for appearing on the outside as good, honest men, but inside they were full of hypocrisy and lawlessness.

Now, show your child the most important way that people are like apples. Cut each apple crosswise and show one half of the apple to your child.

What is on the inside in the center?
[a star]

Every person has a *star* inside of them when they are born, no matter what they look like or the circumstances of their birth. This *star* represents their character and their God-given talents and gifts. It should remind us that we are valuable because we are created in God's image and He has confirmed our value by asking His Son to die for us. Each of us is unique and gifted. Just as we often put a star (*) beside an important point that we want to remember, use the star inside the apple to help your children remember that they have great value, no matter what society may say. The world puts so much emphasis on how we look, that sometimes it's hard to remember that what's most important is what's on the **inside**.

It's important to teach our children about the value of service. Encouraging children to use their talents and gifts to serve God and others will help them to feel better about themselves and to impact their world in a positive way. Show the picture of Mother Teresa to your child.

Mother Teresa was an excellent example of a servant lifestyle. *Was she pretty (by the world's standards)? Was she admired and respected? Why?* She was a perfect example of the value of inner beauty! She was sold out to God and served the needs of others with her God-given talents and gifts.

Scriptures to Consider

Matthew 20:26, I Peter 3:3-4

You can give a boost to your child's self-worth by becoming a better listener. Stop what you are doing and give your full attention and eye contact when your teen wants to speak to you. Ask for his/her opinion about things. The underlying message is, *"You are valuable to me!"*

Many books have been written on building your child's self-worth. This area is very critical—educate yourself so that your child can enjoy a healthy self-worth.

EMOTIONAL NEEDS

We all long to be loved and to love others. Most of the young women that I counseled with at the crisis pregnancy center were looking for love and trying to love their boyfriends through sexual intimacy. In a desperate attempt to feel loved, they often compromised their family values, their sense of morality, their long term goals and finally their whole-person health. Eventually, they found their way to the front door of the center. Frightened, alone and disillusioned, they were now faced with the reality of their decision to use sex to meet their needs for love. Boys are no exception. They have the same longings. Let's not stereotype boys as using sex primarily to satisfy their hormonal urges. There are times when this is true for both sexes. The bottom line is that we all need love and all want to know that we are capable of loving others.

We also have a basic need for security in relationships. While teaching *CREATING POSITIVE RELATIONSHIPS*, I was amazed to find that even sixth graders recognized their need for security. I would ask them: "What do you feel you need the most in a relationship?" They would respond with answers that included honesty and trust. Having security in a relationship means there is safety in the relationship. The other person can be trusted to be honest with their feelings and committed to the relationship. People will be dishonest and uncommitted, but we all desire relationships that are trustworthy and secure.

Often when the emotional needs for love and security are not being met within the family structure, adolescents and teens will use sexual activity as a means to meet those needs. While hearing the family history of a client at the center, many times I would learn that the girl's father was either absent, neglectful or abusive. This seems to support studies that link a teen's sexual vulnerability with dysfunctional family relationships. Young people want to know if they are attractive to the opposite sex. Attentive fathers and mothers can encourage their children by expressing honest admiration.

Sexual intimacy can provide feelings of warmth, love and security. However, the teen who is using sex to satisfy unmet needs for love and security will find only *temporary* satisfaction until the next sexual experience. This type of behavior can lead to sexual promiscuity.

Ultimately, we must all come to realize that our deepest needs for love and security must be brought back to Him. Imperfect people will never be able to fully satisfy our deepest longings. Getting in touch with this truth frees us from the frustration that accompanies unmet expectations of human love. We release those whom we have demanded to be our perfect lovers and are more able to offer unconditional love to them in the process.

Let's Take A Closer Look...

Read the following situations to your child and discuss the questions to illustrate how the need for love and security can lead to sexual involvement.

John is the youngest in his family. His brother and sister went to college by earning scholarships. He is an average student who has very little confidence in himself and doesn't feel that his parents love him for who he is. He hides his true feelings and feels very lonely. He has a girlfriend that really seems to care about him. He can even talk to her about some of his feelings and his dreams. He has been thinking more about wanting to have a sexual relationship with her.

Sue's parents are divorced and her father lives 400 miles away from her. She hardly ever gets to see him. She has no brothers or close male friends. She really wonders what guys think of her—is she attractive, desirable? She's had a couple of boyfriends. She's been getting more physical with her latest boyfriend and figures that they will probably have sex soon.

Sandy's been thinking about having sex with her boyfriend so she could get pregnant. She has always loved babies. Lately, she feels like she and her boyfriend are growing apart... having a baby together would surely bring them close again. Besides, her family is all messed up, nobody loves her, and a baby would give her some of that love she is missing. They think that she is just a kid, but she'd be a good mother.

What are the emotional needs that John, Sue and Sandy may be trying to have met by having a sexual relationship?
[need for love, security, closeness, approval, somebody to love]

What can they do to avoid using sex to meet their emotional needs?
[turn to God in prayer, participate in *Bible* study and fellowship to grow in the knowledge of His perfect love for us, communicate true feelings to parents, get counseling help if needed, build self-confidence by joining a team, club or developing a talent, find some good friends for companionship]

SOCIAL NEEDS

God created us for relationship—first with Himself and then with others. Our relationship with God directly affects our relationship with others. If our vertical relationship with God is out of balance, our relationships with others will fall short of God's design. Experiencing healthy, loving relationships is fundamental to our happiness in life. We want to know that we belong to someone or something—that is why our relationship with God and the family structure is essential. A sense of belonging helps preserve the identity of a struggling adolescent. Young people who do not feel they belong to God nor feel a part of a loving, supportive family may be drawn to an undesirable peer group to meet their need for belonging. This can be observed in the large numbers of teens who are persuaded to join gangs or cults.

It is normal for adolescents and teens to identify more with their peers than with their parents. Teens desperately desire the approval and acceptance of their peers. The need for peer approval is so intense that they will often compromise their values, their desires and their goals to be accepted by their peers. At the same time they are drawing closer to their peers, they are pulling away from their parents. Parents need to consciously strive to provide love, security and family togetherness. This is difficult because often teens want to spend more time with their friends than with their family. Set aside at least one evening or a partial day as family time and guard it as sacred. If teenage rebellion becomes a problem, look for a compromise. Don't be afraid to seek some professional counseling. Sometimes, households can become real battlefields, and family togetherness becomes impossible. It is helpful to seek the counsel of someone you respect who can give you an objective opinion. Many times a teen does not appreciate family unity until they have left for college. Your sincere efforts in this area will pay off in the long run.

How do you respond when your teen seems to be drawn to a less desirable peer group? What if your son brings home a friend with a mohawk haircut and tattoos over every inch of his body? Or your daughter's new friend looks like the wild side of MTV? These are tough issues to tackle. Keep communicating and open your heart and your home to your children and to their peers. Provide opportunities for your child to connect with a positive peer group through school, church or community activities. If you sense that your teen may be identifying with a dangerous group of peers, seek some professional counsel. Pray earnestly for your teen to be drawn to Christian peers and to seek God's help to resist temptation.

Studies indicate that the #1 reason teenagers become involved sexually is because of peer pressure. We can alleviate some of that pressure by encouraging spiritual growth and by providing loving, supportive relationships at home. Chapter 4 will address ways to use peer pressure to have a positive impact in your child's life.

Scriptures to Consider

Proverbs 13:20

LET'S TAKE A CLOSER LOOK...

Read the following situations to your child and discuss the questions to illustrate how the need for belonging and acceptance by peers can lead to sexual involvement.

Julie is not satisfied with her friends. She would rather be included in the popular group that everyone looks up to. They have parties on weekends and seem to be more grown up. She managed to get herself invited to one of their parties. There were no parents around, and some of the guys and girls were pairing off and going into the bedrooms. One of the guys was flirting with Julie and she ended up losing her virginity that night.

Bill's parents are workaholics—they are never around and allow him to do whatever he wants. He doesn't like to be at home by himself, so he's always looking for some action. He's made some new friends who are on the fast track—drinking, drugs, sex. He knows he's heading for trouble, but who cares anyhow? It just feels good to have someone to hang out with, and he's old enough to handle the things they do.

Identify the reasons Julie and eventually Bill have gotten involved sexually.
[popularity and acceptance, peer pressure, loneliness, dysfunctional family, need for belonging, lack of love, boredom]

How can these teens get their needs met without misusing sex?
[seek God's help and learn about becoming a part of God's family, get counseling help for themselves and their families; join clubs, teams, church youth groups or other positive peer groups]

SPIRITUAL NEEDS

God is continually drawing us back to Himself. Life in this fallen world is a continual struggle. We are "strangers, aliens" in this world who long for unconditional love, acceptance and intimacy. We go to many dry wells to try to meet our thirst for intimacy. God's design for sexual intercourse (becoming one flesh) is described as a great mystery. Our bodies are God's temple—our sexuality is divinely linked with our spirituality. Satan counterfeits God's beautiful design by offering premarital sex. The need for spiritual intimacy becomes a powerful lure that can trap teens into pursuing sexual relationships. The only way to protect our teens from falling into this trap is to nurture their spiritual understanding. Read and discuss the implications of I Corinthians 6:18-20 and Romans 7:13 from The *MESSAGE* with your teen. I Corinthians 6 says, "Remember that your bodies are created with the same dignity as the body of Christ. In sexual sin we violate the sacredness of our own bodies, these bodies that were made for God-given and God-modeled love, for becoming one with another." Romans 7 says, "Sin is famous for using the good as a cover to tempt me to do what would finally destroy me."[3]

Scriptures to Consider

I Corinthians 3:16, Ephesians 5:31-32

IN SUMMARY

There are a number of reasons why teens become involved sexually. To begin to understand the complexity of sexuality, we must recognize that adolescent sexual behaviors are often motivated by whole-person needs. *Physically*, they need human physical touch. *Mentally,* they have a need for respect, acceptance and approval from others. They also have a desire for knowledge and understanding that enables them to grow in competence and to reach goals in their lives. Emphasizing the importance of character development in lieu of outer appearance, material wealth, supreme intelligence or abilities will help our child to develop a healthy self-worth. Reinforcing their God-given value by modeling self-respect is also very important. In addition, teaching the value of using talents and gifts to serve God and others gives them the ability to have a positive impact on their world. A strong sense of self-worth is vital because it promotes healthy relationships and helps teens to resist negative peer pressure. *Emotionally,* every teen needs to love and to be loved. Security that includes trust, honesty and commitment is an important factor in experiencing successful relationships. Encouraging teens to seek God and ask Him to meet their deepest longings for love and security will free them from the frustration of unmet expectations of human love. It enables them to love others better. Providing love and security in the home will help a teen to avoid using sex to meet these emotional needs. *Socially,* teens need interpersonal relationships that provide them with a sense of belonging and family. At a time when they are identifying more with their peers than their parents, the availability of a positive peer group is essential. *Spiritually,* teens are searching for intimacy—looking for unconditional love and acceptance. If they do not pursue a love relationship with God, they may settle for Satan's counterfeit—premarital sex.

Whole person needs are universal. It has been said that teens are not really looking so much for sexual expression as they are for personal intimacy. Helping our teens to understand their needs and to have them met in more appropriate ways is the first step in encouraging premarital sexual abstinence. We must encourage our children to seek the Lord and give our best effort to meet their needs within our family structure and in our relationship with them.

Chapter 3

"It won't happen to me!"

Whole-Person Consequences

Among the many young women whom I have counseled with in the past ten years, one lovely girl will stay forever etched in my mind. She was a very attractive sixteen-year-old model. When I met her, she was single, several months pregnant and was battling with a nasty case of genital warts. She had been sexually involved with her two previous boyfriends. My heart ached for this sweet girl who was suffering very painful consequences from her decision to include sex in her relationships. If only someone could have helped her to understand that sex does not have to be a part of a dating relationship. She learned too late that her health and her future goals were going to be greatly affected by her choice to become sexually active.

When teens begin to use sex to meet their whole-person needs, there will be detrimental whole-person consequences. Most people readily identify the physical consequences of sexual activity. These consequences are most visible; however, the less visible can be just as devastating.

LET'S THINK ABOUT IT...

"Casual sex can lead to a casualty."

PHYSICAL CONSEQUENCES

How does premarital sexual activity affect our physical health? A teen is at an obvious risk for contracting a sexually transmitted disease or experiencing an unplanned pregnancy. There have been many cases when a teenage girl became pregnant the first time she had intercourse. Teens seem to think that if they are having sex with just one person over a period of time that they are not at risk for contracting a sexually transmitted disease. Many young girls would call our crisis line with frantic questions. They had just experienced intercourse for the first time and they had no idea if they were at risk for pregnancy or disease. Our children need to know the facts about the consequences of sexual activity. They need to understand how their bodies function and how to keep themselves healthy.

Consider the following statistics:

- *Each year, more than one million teens become pregnant.*[4]
- *Of these pregnancies, more than one third end in abortion.*[5]
- *About 70 percent of these teen mothers are unmarried, and more than 40 percent will drop out of school.*[6]
- *Sexually transmitted diseases infect 3 million teenagers annually.*[7]
- *Two-thirds of people with sexually transmitted diseases become infected before age 25.*[8]
- *The Federal Centers for Disease Control estimate that there were between 650,000-900,000 cases of HIV infection nationwide in 1992.*[9]
- *Studies evaluated through 1990 indicated a 69% risk reduction in acquiring HIV with condom use.*[10]
- *There are now 24 million cases of Human Papilloma Virus (HPV), with a higher prevalence among teens.*[11]
- *More teens have chlamydia—a disease that can cause infertility—than any other age group. About a third of all sexually active teens are infected with this disease.*[12]

There are two ways to respond to these frightening statistics. We can respond with fear and hopelessness or we can roll-up our sleeves and equip our children with the hard truth and the answers to the difficult dilemmas they face today. Sometimes we may have to share information that we wish could wait until they're older. If we hesitate too long, our children could become one of these statistics by default. We will be allowing society, peers, media, schools and all other outside influence to educate and shape the thoughts of our children. Our children should receive this information in a format that includes our values and our standards. To do less is an obvious neglect of our children.

Let's Take A Closer Look...

As you begin to discuss with your teen the physical consequences of sexual activity, use the diagram that follows as an important visual. As you glance at the diagram, notice that the virginity choice is shown in a separate box. When teens choose virginity, they are protected from the difficult decisions that are inevitable with sexual intercourse. Instead, the decisions they will be making might include what to do on the weekend, what movie to see, who to go out with, should I get a Big Mac or a Whopper?, etc. This visual can be used as you discuss with your child the physical consequence of an unplanned pregnancy. Use the key on page 57 to help with your discussion.

SEXUALLY ACTIVE?!
DIFFICULT DECISIONS WILL FOLLOW!

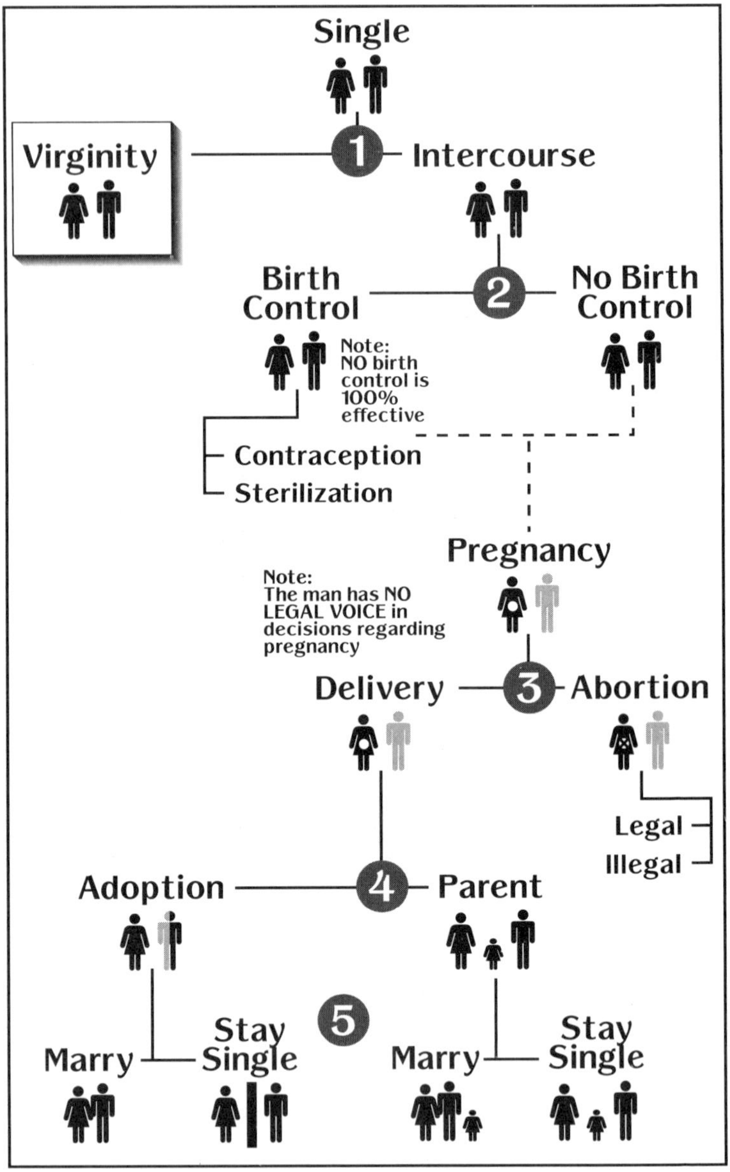

KEY FOR DIAGRAM

1. This diagram shows young people the difficult decisions they will be faced with if they decide to have sexual intercourse instead of saving their gift of sexuality for marriage.
2. If they choose to have intercourse, they must decide if they are going to try to reduce that risk by using a method of birth control or sterilization. **NOTE**: Even with birth control, there still is a risk of pregnancy.
3. They will have to decide, if pregnancy occurs, whether the girl will continue the pregnancy or have an abortion.
   NOTE: The boy has no legal voice in this decision; however, he will be affected by the girl's decision. Also, depending on current law, she may have to decide on a legal or an illegal abortion.
4. If the girl decides to deliver the baby, the next decision is whether to parent or release for adoption. The boy will need to sign release papers for adoption. This can be bypassed by the court if the baby's father cannot be located or doesn't respond to official notification. Laws may vary according to individual states.
5. The next decision is whether the couple will marry or whether the child will be raised by a single parent with the other parent in a supportive role. If the child is released for adoption, will the couple decide to get married, stay single, or break off their relationship?

BIRTH CONTROL

Birth control can be a difficult issue for parents to address. *Should parents take a hard line against premarital sex?* As Christians, we must support the teachings in scripture which clearly define premarital sex as contrary to the will of God.

Should we talk about birth control, just in case? In a 1996 study published by *Family Planning Perspectives,* researchers found that "when mothers took a firm, unequivocal line against premarital sex, had a good relationship with their teenage children and avoided discussing birth control, those children were highly likely to be virgins." Teens with these three factors going for them were 12.5 times more likely to be virgins than teenagers without them. The study's principal author, James Jaccard, a psychology professor at the State University of New York said, "Many parents think adolescence is a time of parental rejection and that they have little influence on teenagers. It becomes very important for parents to open the communication channels because they can have an impact." Parents who proactively discuss birth control methods with their children give the message that they do not believe their children can be sexually abstinent. By initiating a discussion on birth control, well-meaning parents may be inviting their children to experiment with premarital sex. *It is important to promote a high standard of sexual behavior as a worthy, attainable goal.*

On the other hand, parents who learn that their children have chosen to be sexually active—in spite of the moral standards of their parents—may want to consider discussing this dilemma with their family doctor. It must be noted, however, that even the most consistent use of birth control devices will only reduce, not eliminate, the physical consequences of sexual activity. In addition, no birth control device can protect your child from suffering the mental, social, emotional or spiritual consequences of premarital sexual activity.

In the heat of passion, even adult married couples sometimes forego protective measures. It is not realistic to expect teenagers, who routinely forget their vitamins, homework, tennis shoes, chores, etc., to use birth control correctly each and every time. During the course of one year while working at the crisis pregnancy center, I counseled with three girls who were on the pill and still found themselves pregnant.

Let's Think About It...

"The best birth control is self-control."

- *Condoms can fail at least 15.7 percent of the time in preventing pregnancy.*[13]
- *Condoms can rupture—the average breakage rate is 2.5 to 3%.*[14]
- *The FDA standards allow 3-4 holes per 1000 for condom manufacturers.*[15]

- *Only 5% to 40% of sexually active adolescents report that they use condoms consistently.*[16]
- *9.3% to 18.1% of unmarried teenagers on oral contraceptives become pregnant in the first year of use.*[17]
- *2.7 pills per month are missed by the average teenager who uses oral contraceptives; 1 to 2% of women become pregnant every year even if they take the pills daily.*[18]

PREGNANCY

A bright young lady was preparing to go to college when she received the unwelcome news. She was pregnant. She had already broken off the relationship with her baby's father. She realized that her relationship with him was a serious mistake—the course he was choosing for his life was not the same as hers. Abortion was not an option for her because of her strong personal beliefs. She started her first semester in college and began to think about the difficult decisions that she faced. Even though a decision to release for adoption would be very painful, she decided this would be the best decision for herself and her baby. She did not realize that she could only make this decision if her baby's father agreed to sign the papers. Even though he was spending time in jail and was living a reckless life, he had a right to stop the adoption. He invoked his right to oppose the adoption and her choice was narrowed to either she raise the baby or he would seek custody. Wanting to protect her baby from his custody, she dropped out of college and moved back home to become a single parent.

This scenario or similar ones happen every day. In the heat of passion, young people do not think about the serious ramifications of their decision to become sexually active. Lives can be drastically affected by a short moment of pleasure.

Facing an unplanned pregnancy is a very stressful situation that requires difficult decisions. When faced with this situation, it is best to receive counsel from clergy or trained professionals who can help those involved work through the difficult options. Free Christian counseling is available at many crisis pregnancy centers. Every option has its difficulties, particularly for a teenager. The following information is provided to help you to discuss these options with your child. Avoiding the difficulties of an unplanned pregnancy provides a strong argument for premarital abstinence.

Ask your child to think of the possible whole-person consequences of each option. Some examples are given to help you with the discussion.

P E M S

Abortion

Physical — pregnancy terminated, medical risks
Mental — memories of pregnancy and abortion
Emotional — relief, depression, sadness, guilt

Social — rejection or acceptance from peers and others
Spiritual—guilt, responsible to God for ending a life

I have counseled with many women, young and old, who have experienced the pain of an abortion. Abortion is not a happy experience for anyone. For some people it causes grief and guilt that can last for years or a lifetime. Numerous studies reveal that women who have had an abortion experience a high incidence of depression, stress, low self-esteem, suicidal feelings and substance abuse.[19] Others feel it was the best decision for them and seem to have no regrets.

As Christians, we must be careful not to rationalize the truth of abortion. Psalm 139 is very clear that God forms us in the womb and the days of our lives are numbered before we ever live them. Having an abortion deliberately ends a life—in essence we act as God and destroy His creation. In the midst of painful circumstances, our perspective can become skewed. This is why it is very important to consult with a pastor or a Christian counselor.

An abortion cannot be undone. It is a surgical procedure that includes medical risks that can affect a girl's future reproductive health. Many complex feelings surround an abortion for the potential mother and father. Consulting with medical doctors, counselors and clergy is highly recommended. The pregnant teen must make a decision she can live with for the rest of her life. Parents should never force a daughter to have an abortion. This can cause serious conflict in the parent/child relationship indefinitely. A pregnant teen needs parental love and support more than ever. At this time, the potential father has no legal rights with regard to an abortion decision. Gather all of the facts and explore all of the alternatives.

Scriptures to Consider

Psalm 139:13-16, Jeremiah 1:4-5

Parenting

Physical — pregnancy and childbirth risks; for father–financial responsibility
Mental — memories of life before pregnancy; childbirth; adult responsibilities
Emotional — scared, sad, happy, confused
Social — restricted freedom, less friends, school difficulties, ruined reputation
Spiritual — awesome responsibility to nurture a child's spirituality

Most teenage parents would choose to postpone parenthood until later if they would have a second chance. Unfortunately, the awesome responsibility of parenting twenty-four hours a day is not understood until it becomes a reality. Use the following questions to explore the ramifications of teen parenting with your child.

Let's Talk About It...

What are some qualities of a good parent? Which of these qualities would be hard for a teenager to possess?

What is the function of a family?

What is the ideal family situation in which to raise a child?

How would your life change if you became a teen parent?

What is the boy's responsibility as father of the baby?

Choosing to become a teen parent is a challenging option. Fifty percent of teen mothers and 70 percent of teen fathers finish high school.[20] The poverty rate for children living with their single moms is five times greater than the rate for children living with two parents.[21] Laws vary by state, but if paternity is established by a court, a boy may be compelled to financially support his child, regardless of his age. Also, legal charges may be filed against a teen, 16 years or older who has intercourse with a child who is 15 or younger.

<u>**Adoption**</u>

Physical — pregnancy and childbirth risks
Mental — memories of pregnancy and baby
Emotional — difficult to detach from baby, grief, depression, relief; satisfaction of doing what is best for the baby and teen parents
Social — rejection or acceptance from peers and others
Spiritual — peace if God's will is sought; guilt, if God is not included in the decision-making process

I have had the privilege of working with pregnant girls through the adoption process. Since I am an adoptive mother, this seems to offer some comfort and courage to young women contemplating releasing their babies for adoption. It also renews my thankfulness to our daughter's birth mother and my appreciation for her courage.

It takes considerable maturity and support for a teen to release a baby for adoption. It can also be very painful for the potential grandparents. Adoption should be pursued only after much prayer and counseling with a Christian counselor and adoption agency or an adoption attorney. Once again, the birth mother should not be forced or coerced into releasing a baby for adoption. Ultimately, this must be her decision. The birth father will also have to be willing to cooperate.

Adoption can be a very positive, though difficult and painful, option. Several adoption plans are available to help meet the desires of the birth mother and to assist her in the process of letting go. It is helpful for the birth mother to remain in counseling until she has reached a measure of emotional healing. She will need to go through a healthy grief process, as will others who are closely involved with the situation. Remember that God believes in adoption by His example.

Scriptures to Consider

Romans 8:23, 9:4; Ephesians 1:5

MARRIAGE

Experiencing a successful marriage is difficult for two reasonably mature adults. "Shotgun" weddings of the past are not the answer to the teen pregnancy problem. A successful marriage requires spiritual oneness, committed love, unselfish compromise and at times, sheer perseverance. Statistics confirm that it is extremely difficult for teenagers to maintain a marriage relationship. *Sixty percent of young people who marry before the age of twenty will be divorced within five years.* The divorce rate rises to 90 percent if pregnancy is the major reason for marriage.[22]

Often when a couple faces an unplanned pregnancy, the stress of the difficult decisions causes a break up in the relationship. Facing these decisions as a couple undoubtedly will show the maturity and commitment level in the relationship. If the couple desires to marry, it may be wise to postpone marriage until a long term commitment is evident. Facing teen parenthood is very difficult without the pain of a failed marriage. Continually seek God's guidance through prayer and Christian counseling.

SEXUALLY TRANSMITTED DISEASES

Another obvious physical consequence of sexual activity is sexually transmitted diseases (STDs), formerly known as venereal diseases. STDs have become an epidemic today. "STDs are not a stationary group of infections and syndromes; eight new sexually transmitted pathogens have been identified since 1980, including HIV."[23] Twenty years ago, there were two prevalent diseases—syphilis and gonorrhea. Today, experts estimate that there are at least fifty different strains that affect teenagers.[24]

Use the following questions and information to explain the basics of STDs to your child.

Why are there so many more STDs? More sexual activity outside of marriage with more partners is a significant factor in the STD epidemic. In addition, the symptoms for STDs can be very evasive so that people who are infected don't realize that they are contagious. Some of the common symptoms are flu-like symptoms, blisters, poor health, burning during urination and genital discharge. Embarrassment may also cause an infected person to neglect to inform their former or current sexual partners.

Even though STDs affect our physical bodies, they can bring mental, emotional and social consequences as well. Embarrassment, low self-worth, shame, ridicule and rejection are common reactions to contracting an STD.

How do you get an STD? STDs are caused by viruses, bacteria and small organisms. These infections are passed from one person to another through body fluids, primarily sexual fluids and blood or by direct intimate contact. Human Immunodeficiency Virus (HIV) has been found in tears and saliva but there is no current evidence of transmission in this way. HIV can be found in semen (including the first drop of fluid, even before ejaculation) and in vaginal fluids. These fluids must enter from one person into the other person through openings in the body such as the eyes, mouth, vagina, penis, anus, tiny cuts or sores. Teens need to understand that any sexual contact— sexual intercourse and, in some cases, simply touching the infected area can transmit these diseases.

Are they curable? There are three STDs, besides AIDS, that are incurable because they are caused by viruses. Just as colds, the flu, etc. are caused by viruses that antibiotics will not cure, viral STDs are not curable and stay in the body indefinitely with periodic flare-ups. The viral STDs are: Genital Herpes (Herpes Simplex II), Genital Warts (HPV) and Hepatitis. The bad news is that if one of these STDs is contracted during the adolescent/teen years, it will stay with the individual indefinitely. Do not confuse the Herpes

Simplex I virus which causes fever or sun blisters with Herpes Simplex II, the Genital Herpes virus. The blisters are similar, but Genital Herpes is sexually transmitted. The STDs that are caused by bacteria can be treated with antibiotics, although some strains are becoming resistant.

LET'S THINK ABOUT IT...

"An STD is a lousy wedding gift."

What are the potential effects of STDs? Many STDs can cause pelvic inflammatory disease. Pelvic inflammatory disease (PID) is often responsible for infertility and sterility problems. Other potential effects of STD infection are arthritis, heart disease, blindness, risk of certain cancers, a higher risk of AIDS and even death. Females are at significantly greater risk of acquiring STDs and resulting health complications than males.[25]

Will condoms give protection from STDs? *A condom, when properly used, will give some protection but cannot eliminate the risk of STDs.* It is not realistic to expect that adolescents and teenagers will use a condom properly and consistently with every sexual experience. Experts agree that condoms are useless in the prevention of some diseases including HPV which infects over 40 percent of some groups and is the precipitating agent for the vast majority of cancers of the cervix, vulva, vagina, and penis. Several studies have shown that condoms do not protect against this virus.[26] The Department of Health and Human Services instructs condom manufacturers to include in their instructions the following: *"When used properly, the latex condom may prevent the transmission of many sexually transmitted diseases... It cannot eliminate the risk. For maximum protection, it is important to follow the accompanying instructions. There should be a warning about the loss of protection resulting from improper use."*[27] The Centers for Disease Control and Prevention states, "For infectious agents spread from lesions rather than fluids, condoms may offer less protection because areas of skin not covered by the condom may be infectious or vulnerable to infection."[28] An evaluation of all available studies through 1990 of heterosexual couples where one partner had HIV and the other did not found that the risk of acquiring HIV was reduced by about 69 percent when condoms were used.[29]

Refer to the *APPENDIX* on pages 177-189 for more specific information on the "10 MOST COMMON STDs." Spend some time with your child (according to age appropriateness) reviewing the information. Utilize your local library to gather more information on AIDS and to spend more time discussing this frightening epidemic.

Let's Think About It...

"Will 'safe sex' or 'saved sex' create a more trusting relationship with your future spouse?"

Let's Take A Closer Look...

Draw the following diagram to explain to your child how STDs can be unknowingly spread over the course of several years and several partners. Sometimes teens will think they are safe as long as they are having a sexual relationship with only one person during a given period of time.

virgin

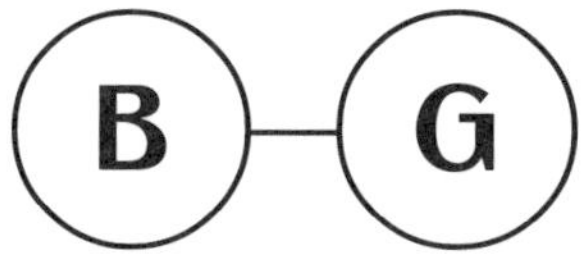

non-virgin

- Begin with two circles: **B** and **G**.
- **B** was a virgin, but his girlfriend had a sexual relationship with a previous boyfriend.
- The previous boyfriend had intercourse with a girlfriend that he dated for two years and another girl he had met at a party.
- The party girl had a sexual relationship with her former boyfriend.
- That boyfriend had dated two girls over a four year period and had a sexual relationship with both of them.
- One of those girls found out that she contracted an STD. She got treatment from her doctor but didn't tell her ex-boyfriend.

How many of these young people could have an STD?
[all of them]

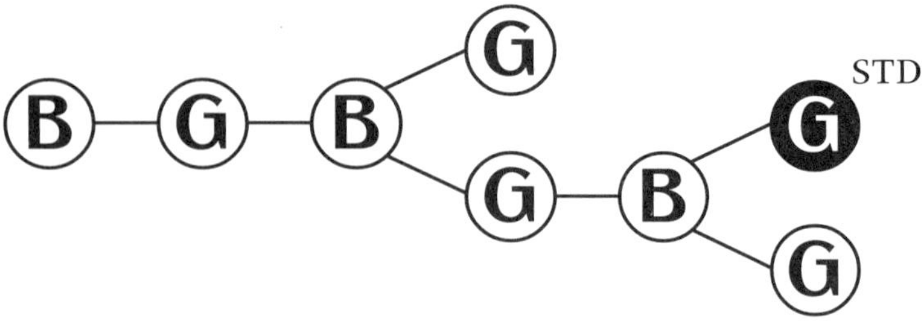

STDs are easily passed from one person to another. Because it takes some STDs as long as ten years to manifest symptoms (HIV) and some have no symptoms at all, *when you have sex with a person, it is like you are having sex with every partner he/she has had sex with in the last ten years.* The only sure way of protecting yourself from an STD is to practice a mutually faithful monogamous (one person) relationship. This does not include "serial monogamy"—having a sexual relationship with one person until the relationship ends, then moving on to another, then another, etc.

Let's Think About It...

"Your lover's sexual history is <u>your</u> sexual history. How romantic!"

MENTAL CONSEQUENCES

Because our sexuality affects our whole person, there will be mental consequences, in addition to physical consequences, from sexual involvement. Often the mental consequences are less visible, but they can be just as painful.

Our brains function as incredible computers; however, some thoughts can never be deleted. *Powerful memories can linger for years.* People never forget the day or the person involved when they lost their virginity. Years later they may want to forget, but the memories live on. In a marriage relationship, comparisons can creep into the mind causing guilt and shame. Spouses may find it difficult to forgive each other for past sexual experiences and may struggle with jealousy and trust issues.

Let's Think About It...

"If it is easy to remember a kiss, will memories of intimate sexual touch be more vivid?"

CREATIVE DEMONSTRATION

Make the following points with this demonstration:

- *Not setting limits of affection allows flames of passion to ignite.*
- *Premarital sex complicates a relationship and introduces new feelings.*
- Feelings may fade, but powerful memories remain after a sexual relationship.

One creative way to illustrate the consequence of lingering memories with your child is to use some puff-out proof candles. Tell a short story about two teens who fell in love and because they had not set any limits of physical affection, they eventually became involved sexually. (Light the candles.) Their relationship seemed to change after they started having sex. They both became more jealous and possessive. She worried about getting pregnant, and they didn't talk about their feelings much anymore. Each time they were together, they spent most of their time getting physical. They thought their love would last forever, but eventually their romance grew cold and they broke up. (Blow out the candles when the relationship breaks up.) Both began new relationships, thinking that the old relationship was out of their lives. They began to realize that this was not true. (The candles continue to reignite even after you keep trying to blow them out.) Powerful memories of a past sexual relationship will keep coming back again and again.

• • •

The sexual bond is very powerful. As mentioned earlier, this is a spiritual mystery. It provides intimacy and closeness between two people in amazing ways. Certainly, we expose the most intimate parts of our physical body. In addition, we are exposing ourselves emotionally, mentally, socially and spiritually. Sexual intercourse can bring great pleasure and deep fulfillment to a loving relationship. This partially explains why *sexual bonding can fool a person into believing there is a strong commitment in the relationship.* Once sexual intimacy is included in a premarital relationship, the focus of the relationship often centers on the physical aspect of the relationship because it provides wonderful, close feelings. The couple spends less time communicating and getting to know each other in other areas of their lives.

Sexual intimacy can also affect one's self-image. People sometimes begin to think that their personal worth is based upon sexual competence or availability. Each time a relationship ends, the person begins to think, *"What's wrong with me? Why doesn't anyone love me enough to stay with me?"* This desperate attempt to find acceptance and self-worth can lead to sexual promiscuity. The downward spiral of low self-worth continues.

Everyone has personal dreams and goals for their lives. Premarital sex can delay or destroy these dreams and goals because of unplanned pregnancy, disease or heartache. It can cause stress and worry about the future. A young person who continually worries about the possibility of pregnancy, disease, a broken relationship, the reaction of parents, spiritual guilt, etc. is not free to concentrate on enjoying life today. Many times schoolwork or other productive activities are affected which can add more conflict to the life of a teenager. *Dreams of college, career, family and carefree days of youth are replaced with difficult adult decisions and responsibilities.*

Scriptures to Consider

I Corinthians 6:18-20

EMOTIONAL CONSEQUENCES

Sex, outside of a committed marriage relationship, can introduce new, complicated feelings. Since sexual intercourse exposes the most intimate parts of a person, fear of the breakdown of trust is likely to occur. For example, a person subconsciously begins to think, *"I have given all I can to this relationship and have exposed all of myself. What if my partner betrays me? Are my secrets safe with my partner? Since my partner is willing to have a sexual relationship outside of a marriage commitment, is there less commitment in our sexual bond?"* Because of our need for love and security, jealousy, possessiveness and fear of breaking up can begin to dominate the relationship. These insecure feelings will bring continual conflict in the relationship.

The break-up of a teen relationship is almost inevitable. *What kinds of feelings remain after the relationship has ended?* The more emotional involvement invested in the relationship, the more painful the parting. Feelings of being used, betrayed and rejected are common. Emotional pain, anger, embarrassment and sadness will be more intense if the relationship was sexual. We cannot protect our teens from the pain of broken relationships. We can encourage them to remain sexually abstinent to minimize their hurt feelings.

Let's Talk About It...

What's the likelihood of adolescent/teen relationships staying together until marriage?

How do people feel when a relationship is broken and they are dumped for another?

How might sexual involvement intensify the emotional feelings during a relationship and when the relationship ends?

If premarital sex is contrary to the moral values of the family, what other emotions might be experienced?
[guilt, shame]

CREATIVE DEMONSTRATION

Make the following points with this demonstration:

- Sexual intercourse creates a powerful whole-person bond between two people.
- This bond may fool you into thinking there's more to the relationship than there really is.
- When the relationship is broken, there will be emotional pain and possible long-term effects.
- Sex before marriage weakens the marital bond.
- Sexual intercourse loses its meaning through promiscuity.

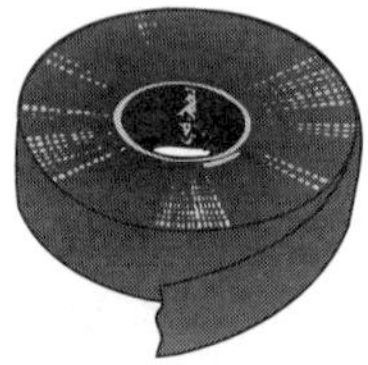

Use a piece of sticky duct tape to illustrate the consequences of premarital sexual bonding.

Ask your child for permission to place the tape on his/her arm. (If your child does not want to cooperate, use your own arm.) Explain that just as the glue on the tape is a powerful bonding agent between the tape and the arm, sexual intercourse is like God's glue that bonds two people together in a most powerful, intimate way. *What happens when that bond is broken?* (Pull the tape off of the arm.) *Ouch!* It hurts! The same thing happens when a sexual bond is broken—there is emotional and mental pain. Look at the backside of the tape. *What do you see?* [hair] Just as some of the hair stuck to the tape, a part of ourselves will always stay with the person we have sexually bonded with and a part of them with us. *What else may stick with you?* [memories, STDs, pregnancy] Now, put the tape on the arm again (or another arm). This time when the tape is pulled off, it doesn't stick as well so it doesn't hurt as badly. In the same way as the tape lost its stickiness, the sexual bond will lose its purpose—the ability to strengthen and keep the relationship together. It doesn't hurt as badly to end a relationship and to begin another. If we misuse our sexuality by bonding with a person then breaking up and bonding with another person, sexual intercourse can lose its meaning and value. It can become just a physical act, something pleasurable and fun to do. It might temporarily provide us with pleasure, but sooner or later, it will not meet our need for intimacy.

LET'S THINK ABOUT IT...

"Sexual promiscuity is a counterfeit of the original beauty and purpose of sexual intimacy."

SOCIAL CONSEQUENCES

Because we are relational beings, our social life will always be very important. We all want to belong to a family or a group—we need to feel connected within a community of people.

How does premarital sex affect our relationships? Because sexual intimacy complicates a teen relationship, break-ups are likely. All of the consequences previously discussed can bring stress into the relationship. Teens engaged in adult activities inherit adult-size problems. Most of their relationships are not mature enough to weather the difficulties that occur.

Some teens make the initial error of thinking they will gain more acceptance and popularity by becoming sexually active. Instead, the sexually active teen might develop a bad reputation for being sexually promiscuous. Teens with higher moral standards will begin to avoid or reject the teen whose reputation has been marred. *This peer rejection further destroys the self-respect of the hurting teen.* When physical consequences occur, such as pregnancy and disease, former friends may scatter. The troubled teen is without companionship and no longer has a social life.

Let's Think About It...

"The time to think about your reputation is before you have one."

Scriptures to Consider

Proverbs 22:1

Parents who trust their teens to control their sexual behavior and then realize their teens are sexually active, might find it difficult to reestablish trust in their relationship. After discovering the truth, they may react by trying to control the teen and give less independence. This can result in more teen rebellion and more sexual activity. Parents will have to struggle with their own feelings of hurt, anger and disappointment if their children choose a different path contrary to their family values. Parents should seek God's help and outside counsel, if necessary, to work through these feelings, so they can love and accept their teens in spite of their behavior.

SPIRITUAL CONSEQUENCES

Because sex outside of a marriage covenant is contrary to God's law, disobedience results in spiritual consequences.

Isaiah 59:2 says that our sin separates us from God, His face is hidden from us and our prayers are hindered. We experience guilt and shame and begin to shut God out of our lives. As a result of his sin, David vividly describes his anguish in Psalm 38. God loves us and will discipline us. He has given sexual expression His parameters to protect us from harm and to provide His best for us. If we choose the path of destruction, we will reap what we sow. God will not spare us from the consequences of our wrong choices. There will be no peace in our lives until we confess, repent and turn from our sin. Praise God that He has provided a way through Christ for forgiveness and restoration.

Scriptures to Consider

Psalm 38, Isaiah 59:2, Galatians 5:19-23, Ephesians 5:3, Hebrews 12:7-11, I John 1:9

IN SUMMARY

Understanding the whole-person consequences of premarital sex can give adolescents and teenagers the desire to save their *gift of sexuality* for a committed marriage relationship.

Unplanned pregnancy, abortion and sexually transmitted diseases affect the physical health of teens. Teens are notorious for touting the *"It won't happen to me"* mindset. Statistics continue to confirm that they are very wrong, sometimes *dead* wrong. Painful memories, low self-image and delayed or lost goals often accompany premarital sexual activity. Feelings that include anger, embarrassment, sadness, guilt and feeling used are also common. Suffering through numerous broken relationships, rejection and the loss of trust, teens can find themselves wondering what ever happened to their carefree days of youth. The loss of inner spiritual peace will surround each one of these painful consequences. A teen's relationship with God is stifled and eventually, the reality of "what we sow, we shall reap" prevails.

The consequences of premarital sex are serious and can be life threatening. Since it is our desire that our children live fulfilled, healthy lives, we must do everything we can to help them to make responsible, healthy decisions. As much as we would like to, we cannot make their decisions for them. Ultimately, we will have to live with their choices, just as they will have to live with the consequences of their decisions. As previously stated, we are responsible to our children—to love them, to teach them, to provide for them, to discipline them. We are not responsible for the choices they make. If we do our best to provide for their needs, we should not blame ourselves if our children choose to take a different path than we would desire for them. They will have to suffer the consequences of their choices, but they will continue to need our prayers, love and support.

Chapter 4

"Grow Up!"

Whole-Person Maturity

Maturity. It's *hard* work. Webster defines *mature* as "having attained a final or desired state." Maturity is a lifetime process that takes considerable effort. The benefits of whole-person maturity are endless. One of the biggest misunderstandings about sexuality is that once our body is grown up—physically mature, we think that we are ready to *use it*. That kind of thought process is the seed for unrestrained sexual activity. Once again, because our sexuality affects our whole person, we must begin to work on whole-person maturity. Christ is our perfect example. Luke 2:52 says that "Jesus grew in wisdom, stature, and in favor with God and man" (physically, mentally, emotionally, socially and spiritually).

PHYSICAL MATURITY

Physical maturity is almost an automatic process. As long as we are reasonably healthy, our bodies grow and develop. Physical development occurs at a different pace for each person. Our pituitary gland, which is located at the base of the brain, is in charge of this growth process. This gland is like our own personal calendar that decides when things start blooming. Adolescents may have anxiety because they are developing ahead of or behind their peers. Girls begin showing the physical signs of puberty earlier than boys. The average age at which children reach puberty has dropped dramatically over the past century.

Adolescents need lots of support and encouragement during this stage of their lives. This is not always easy because often they are grouchy, uncooperative, hormonal and generally confused about growing up. Sometimes they try to act like adults, while at other times, they want to be coddled like children. This time of adolescence can be a real test of parental patience. It certainly will be a test of *our maturity!*

While society is busy brainwashing our children about the importance of beautiful or athletic bodies and sexual attractiveness, we must be very diligent to reassure them of their own uniqueness and value based upon their character.

LET'S THINK ABOUT IT...

"Did you ever see a healthy adult with the body of a 12-year-old?"

MENTAL MATURITY

An 11-year-old sixth-grader came to the crisis pregnancy center for help. She was an adolescent who had been sexually active for one year and had now conceived a baby. She refused to get an abortion or release her baby for adoption. She wanted to parent her baby. She had some pet baby rabbits that she thought were so cute—her baby would be another cute little pet. Her body was physically mature enough to conceive a child. However, mentally, she still was an 11-year-old sixth-grader.

What is mental maturity? Mental maturity requires *thinking* about the consequences of our decisions before we make them. Mental maturity says, "How is this decision going to affect my life?" This is a lifetime process and not an easy concept to get across to the

"It's not going to happen to me!" adolescent/teenager. Children need to learn when they are young that every decision has a corresponding consequence—good or bad. Sometimes it is hard to allow our children to suffer the consequences of their decisions. It is so easy for merciful mom or dad to intervene to save their child from suffering the pain of an irresponsible decision. The reality is that when we rescue our children from legitimate consequences, we are delaying the maturity process for them. Mom and dad will not always be available to rescue them. Our goal as parents is to equip them, so they can become responsible, caring adults. *Rescuing them from consequences keeps them in the infant stage of mental maturity and can give the impression that they cannot make it through life without us.* Suffering consequences encourages maturity.

Somehow the call for immediate gratification which beckons them to feel good now and don't worry about tomorrow is much more inviting than the discipline of evaluating decisions. *"Have it your way!"* and *"Grab all the gusto!"* constantly lures them into society's value*less* system. These are the days of instant everything—from coffee and fast-food to dry-cleaning, banking and even drive-up divorce. Our children have to learn to swim upstream and we need to be right behind them giving our applause. *Don't give up.* Society will be happy to raise your children for you according to *its* standards.

Discuss with your child the meaning of immediate gratification. Look at each word—immediate means instant or right now and gratification means a source of satisfaction or pleasure. *IMMEDIATE GRATIFICATION = INSTANT SATISFACTION OR PLEASURE.* A person who is seeking immediate gratification is saying, "I want to feel good now!" with no thought for tomorrow. One way to explain to your child that seeking immediate gratification is immature behavior is by giving the example of a hungry infant. When the baby's hungry, is he willing to wait for the next feeding while you finish watching your TV program? No! The baby wants to satisfy the hunger pain right now and is not willing to wait. A baby has no maturity to wait to satisfy his desires. As the baby grows up, he will have to learn to delay gratification. Our adolescents and teens also need to learn that delaying gratification is a process of maturity that takes effort but brings future benefits.

Oswald Chambers, whose writings are published in *My Utmost For His Highest* says, "Temptation comes to me, suggesting a possible shortcut to the realization of my highest goal, it does not direct me toward what I understand to be evil, but toward what I understand to be good." Sexual purity is God's highest goal for our children in the area of sexuality. The temptation of immediate gratification appears to be good at the time, but is a shortcut to God's best for their lives.[30]

Let's Take A Closer Look...

Give the following assignment. Ask your children to write down all of the immediate gratification messages they hear or see through TV commercials, music, billboards or magazines for a week. When the assignment is completed, talk about it with them and reward them with a favorite meal or night out.

Setting goals and making plans to reach those goals encourages the process of mental maturity. As children identify goals and attain their goals, they begin to satisfy their need for competence and significance. Allow your children to determine their goals. Some parents try to reach their own unattained goals by insisting their children adapt these goals. Guide them by suggesting goals that are challenging, yet attainable, according to their strengths and interests. At the same time, be careful to maintain the delicate balance between what they do and who they are. It is easy to fall into the trap of attaching value to performance, rather than character, by stressing success at all cost. It is good to affirm achievement, but be sure to also recognize an honest effort.

Ask your child to write down some short-term and long-term goals. Using your child's goals, brainstorm some plans to attain these goals. Keep this process simple and fun.

Continue with the discussion by exploring what could happen to the goals if they opt for immediate gratification.

EXAMPLE:
Short-term goal — Get an A in math.
Long-term goal — Become a engineer.
Immediate gratification — have fun, don't study, do homework later, etc.
Consequence — both goals lost or delayed

Setting goals and having a strategy to reach those goals are very important aspects of mental maturity.

LET'S THINK ABOUT IT...

"If you aim at nothing, you'll hit it every time."

Scriptures to Consider

Philippians 3:14

CREATIVE DEMONSTRATION

Make the following points with this demonstration:

- Mental maturity requires thinking about decisions before acting—considering future consequences.
- Goals will be delayed or lost if decisions are based on immediate gratification.
- Circumstances may require adjustments if one plans to attain goals.
- It is important to establish an abstinence goal.

Use a mop to demonstrate the importance of goal setting, delaying immediate gratification and the possibility of lost/delayed goals when teens become involved sexually.

The mop represents your child's life: the handle represents today and the scrubbing end of the mop represents her goals. Ask your child to try to balance the mop handle vertically on the palm of her hand. After balancing the mop, ask what enabled her to accomplish this feat. [Keep her eye on the scrubbing end of the mop, adjust her hand back and forth to balance.] This is also true with our lives. If we want to keep our life in balance and reach our goals, we must keep our eyes on our goals as we make our decisions. If we have no goals, our lives will have no direction. Just as we had to adjust the mop to keep it from falling, sometimes we may have to adjust our plans in order to reach our goals. For example, a goal to attend college may be delayed if there are financial difficulties, strict academic requirements, health problems, etc. It's important to have several plans for reaching our goals if the first plan needs adjustment.

Now ask your child to try to balance the mop by looking straight ahead at the handle, (focused on today, she cannot look up) and standing still (cannot move her hand). This time the mop will fall. If we just focus on what we want today (immediate gratification), our goals will be delayed or lost. In the area of sexuality, if we fall for immediate gratification, with no thought about how our behavior will affect our lives and goals, we are headed for trouble! Personalize this demonstration by using your child's goals and discussing how these goals could be affected by premarital sexual activity. In addition to the physical consequences, don't forget the mental, emotional, social and spiritual consequences that could impact her short or long-term goals.

• • •

A young unmarried couple was at home alone watching a romantic movie. They had not talked about setting any limits in their physical affection because they didn't think that it was necessary. They had not planned to have sexual intercourse anytime soon. However, as the evening progressed, their passion escalated. With no one around to interrupt their activity, one thing led to another and their passion culminated in sexual intercourse.

Many young people experience sexual intercourse for the first time by accident. Good intentions are not sufficient to control sexual desires and maintain sexual abstinence until marriage. Now is the time to set a goal and to develop a plan for sexual abstinence. If teens wait until they are faced with the decision, it will be very difficult. Feelings and hormones will be paving the way to immediate gratification.

An essential part of maintaining an abstinence goal is setting limits on physical affection in a premarital relationship *(drawing a line of affection)*. Talking about this before your child is in a dating relationship and encouraging a commitment to an established standard will be very helpful. Begin this discussion by drawing a set of stair steps and labeling as shown below:

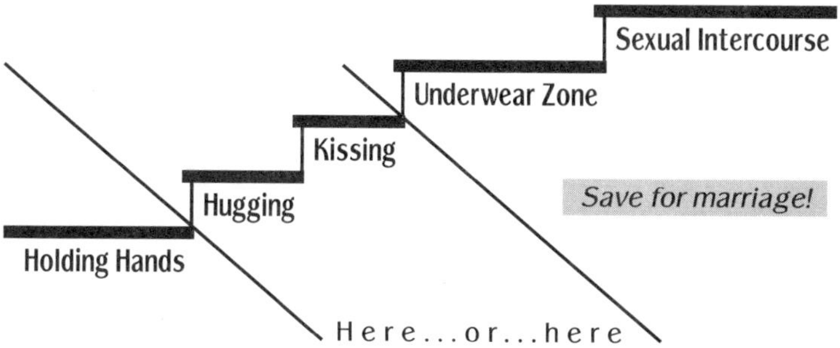

In a dating relationship, there are various levels of physical touch that can eventually lead to sexual intercourse. Our bodies are wired so that as we move from one level to the next level, there is an escalation of desire for more intimate touch. Our sexual desires are normal and healthy and are not shameful. Because these desires are powerful, we must learn to control them or they will control us. There is a natural progression that occurs from one level of physical touch to the next level.

Steps of Affection

- ***Holding Hands*** — *The first level of physical touch is very exciting. This excitement can begin to wane after a time leading to a desire for more intimate physical touch.*
- ***Kissing*** — *There are different types of kissing, from the little peck (grandma's kiss) to a deeper level of intimacy with French or deep kissing.*

- **Underwear Zone** — *The underwear zone is a simple way to describe intimate touch on the parts of our bodies that are covered by underwear. This touch can be on the outside of clothes or directly on the body. It is important to "draw a line of affection"* **before** *the underwear zone. Sexual excitement will peak and there will be a powerful desire to have intercourse. It becomes difficult and uncomfortable to shut down at this point. In addition, there is a risk of contracting an STD with this intimate level of sexual foreplay. Other consequences of the underwear zone should be stressed. Most teen relationships will eventually break up. Teens may experience a range of negative, hurtful emotions when they face their "ex." This is a good time to review the mental, emotional, social and spiritual consequences discussed in the previous chapter.*

Some teens want to avoid intercourse but think they can experiment in the underwear zone without any detrimental effects. Shutting down the natural progression of sexual excitement leaves one feeling frustrated, dissatisfied, and sometimes depressed. In addition, women particularly may have difficulty reaching a sexual climax later in marriage when their minds have programmed their bodies to shut down before intercourse. This is an example of how our minds are a very important part of our sexuality.

Hormones and feelings will lead us to a natural progression if we are not committed to a stopping point. The longer teens wait to experience each level of affection, the more special each level becomes to them. As in the tape demonstration, if a person becomes overly generous with their physical affection, it will become less meaningful to them and to others. Many teens fall into sexual play and intercourse, even though they have good intentions of waiting until they're older or married. Because physical affection is pleasurable and desirable, sometimes the best deterrent for a young person is the realization that there is a risk of disease when progressing past the kissing level of physical affection.

CREATIVE DEMONSTRATION

Make the following points with this demonstration:

- Good intentions cannot keep us out of trouble.
- If we have not firmly set limits of affection, we can be drawn into sexual foreplay and intercourse before we realize what is happening.
- There is a natural progression that leads to sexual intercourse.
- It is possible to stop the progression, but it will take a fast leap out of the situation.

FREDDIE THE FROG

Use the story of Freddie the Frog to explain how natural progression of physical affection can lead us into trouble.

Tell a story of Freddie the Frog who is looking for a cool pool of water to take a swim. A sneaky fellow who wants frog legs for lunch is hanging out trying to figure out how to get Freddie into his pot of boiling water. At first, Freddie accepts his invitation and jumps into the pot of water for refreshment. *Yeow!* Because the water is boiling, he immediately jumps back out. Eventually, his trust in Mr. Sneaky is restored, and he carefully climbs into a second kettle of *cool* water. However, he is unaware that Mr. Sneaky is slowly turning up the heat while he is relaxing in the water. (Remember, frogs are amphibians so their bodies can adapt to their environment.) Before long, Freddie reaches a slow boil and (you guessed it), he becomes Mr. Sneaky's lunch!

The same thing can happen to teens who have not consciously *"drawn their line"* before they are involved in a relationship. They are slowly lured by their hormones and feelings into hot water—sexual play or intercourse.

LET'S THINK ABOUT IT...

"Make decisions with your head, not your hormones. No one plans to fail, but many fail to plan."

Scriptures to Consider

Proverbs 14:15, Romans 12:1-2

Another aspect of mental maturity is thinking about the signals we are sending to the opposite sex. Boys and girls are drawn to each other initially by physical attractiveness. Personality and interests keep them together in a relationship.

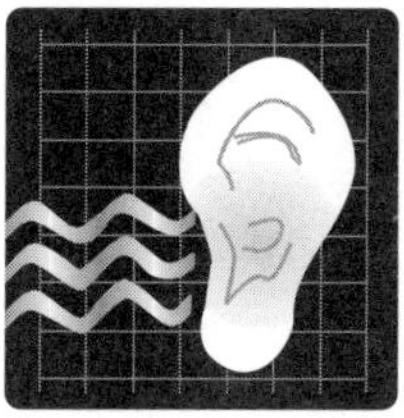

Generally, girls tend have an *ear gate*—they are looking for a guy who listens to them, talks with them and enjoys their companionship. They are especially attracted to a boy who has these attributes. Girls can get caught up in romantic feelings, listening for "I love you." Daughters need to be warned that there are some smooth talkers out there who would love to take advantage of them. They also should be told that boys can be very turned on by their bodies. It is best to have a father or a male friend explain to girls how guys think and the importance of modesty in their clothing choices and the way they act around boys.

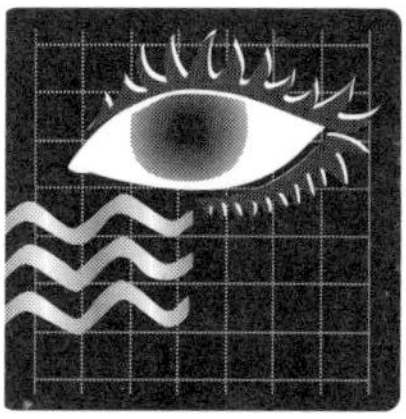

Boys tend to have an e*ye gate*—they are attracted to what they see. Their bodies can begin to respond without any intention on their part. This does not mean that boys are shallow and do not desire a relationship. Boys should be warned that girls will flirt and dress sexy, but that does not necessarily mean they are interested in having a physical relationship. Girls can also be very aggressive with boys. Sexual aggressiveness is promoted and admired by society today. Boys need to know how to handle an aggressive girl without being disrespectful.

As parents, one of the most important ways you can teach your children proper behavior is by modeling it with your spouse or friends of the opposite sex. *Children will do what you do, before they do what you say.* In addition, they really don't care *how much you know* until you show them *how much you care.*

EMOTIONAL MATURITY

Imagine yourself as a parent in the following setting. *Your preschooler is having a temper tantrum in the grocery store because he wants you to buy his favorite junky, sugar-laden cereal and you refuse.* How would you respond?

- *Give in and get the cereal just this one time to save embarrassment.*
- *Smack him on the behind and ignore his screams and the dirty looks of the other frazzled grocery store patrons.*
- *Ignore him and hurriedly finish your grocery shopping.*

- ➢ *Leave all of your groceries and walk out of the store.*
- ➢ *Start screaming at him to shut up and eventually dissolve into tears.*
- ➢ *Never take him to the grocery store again until he grows up.*

Most of us have probably experienced this or a similar situation in our course of parenting. Perhaps we have tried *all of the above* in our efforts to respond. When our adolescents react to situations with emotional outbursts, we must be careful not to respond with our own emotional outbursts.

Emotional maturity is also a lifetime process. How many adults do we see daily who are emotionally *immature*? How often are *we* emotionally immature? When we allow ourselves to lose control of our emotions, we should confess and apologize. If we admit our mistakes, rather than rationalize and try to cover them up, our children will be more likely to listen to our advice. Let's not give the impression that we have *arrived.*

Emotional maturity means that we are in the driver's seat of our feelings—we control them; they do not control us. This is a very difficult task indeed. How do we feel when we let our emotions control us? Give your child some examples from your own life. Use the example of anger, for instance. When we are angry and allow our anger to control us, we usually lash out with hurtful words, or perhaps we express our anger through various forms of destructiveness. We often feel guilty, embarrassed and sorry after such an outburst. Once again, our example as parents will far outweigh our instruction. It truly is a humbling experience to apologize to our children, but the long-term benefits greatly outweigh our momentary discomfort.

Emotional maturity does not mean we should *stuff* our feelings. If we stuff or deny our feelings, they will explode at some point. It's important to give validity to your child's feelings. Don't say, *"That's stupid, you shouldn't feel that way!"* Children should be taught that feelings are okay. Feelings are actually signals that tell us that we need to talk about something that's going on in our heads. It's how we *act* on our feelings that can get us into trouble. In the area of sexuality our feelings are powerful. If we do not develop self-control, we will not be able to maintain a goal of sexual abstinence.

As Christians, we are miraculously equipped to exercise self-control. The Holy Spirit resides in our hearts and freely gives us this attribute. Often, our own sinful nature raises its ugly head and quenches the Spirit. God gives us all we need to live a righteous life.

Scriptures to Consider

Proverbs 25:28, I Corinthians 10:13, Galatians 5:22-23, II Peter 1:3

SOCIAL MATURITY

John, a seventh-grader, is walking down the school hallway with a bunch of his buddies. An overweight, shy sixth-grade girl is walking a few steps in front of them. One of the boys starts making fun of her, hurling all kinds of verbal put downs and crude jokes at her. The other boys quickly join in with the jokes and fun at her expense. John feels sorry for the girl and knows this kind of behavior is wrong, but he doesn't have the courage to stop the tirade. He just laughs along with the crowd.

Ask your child what he or she would do in a similar situation. A good thought to keep in mind is: "What would Jesus do?" We must remember that all people are created in the image of God—they are a part of Him. How we behave toward others is a direct action **against** or **for** God. We must have the Holy Spirit in our hearts to exercise godly respect and love in our relationships. As mentioned earlier, our relationship with God directly affects our relationship with others. If we're having lots of relational problems, perhaps we need to take a hard look at our relationship with God.

Social maturity is more than learning to behave appropriately in social settings. This type of maturity involves how we respond to situations where we interact with people. In simpler terms for adolescents and teens, *how do they respond to peer pressure?* If you have taught your children standards of right and wrong behavior, how do they respond when those standards are challenged in a social setting? To stand up for what they believe and not cave into negative peer pressure requires maturity.

Peer pressure is always with us. Give an example from your own life of adult peer pressure. As mentioned earlier in Chapter 2, studies show that the #1 reason teens become sexually active is peer pressure. One way to help our children learn to stand against negative peer pressure is to do some role-playing with them.

Let's Take A Closer Look...

What would you do or say if...??

Your date tried to coax you into sexual activity by saying the following:

- "If you really love me, you'll show me by giving me all of your love."
- "It will make our relationship stronger and more committed."
- "What could be wrong with something so loving?"
- "I don't feel like going to the game. Let's just go to my house and 'hang out'. My parents are out, so we can do whatever we feel like."
- "Let's stop at this party. My friend told me that it should be a great time—her parents are gone and her boyfriend is bringing the beer."

Use the following refusal formula from *CREATING POSITIVE RELATIONSHIPS* to help your teen remember how to say NO to an invitation to trouble. Practice using the formula with the situations previously mentioned and any others that might occur.

The CPR "Life-Saving" Formula

C	**Communicate it:**	*Say NO to the idea and state why.*
P	**Promote it:**	*Come up with an alternative plan of action.*
R	**Run with it:**	*Stick to the alternative plan and leave the door open for the other person to follow.*

Remind your teen that:

"I want you."
doesn't mean *"I want the best for you."*

"I need you."
doesn't mean *"I'll be there for you."*

"I'll be careful."
doesn't mean *"I care about your feelings."*

"You're so cool."
doesn't mean *"I love you for who you are."*

This would be a good time to share any personal experiences (good or bad) that you faced as a teenager.

Children need to be taught standards of right and wrong so they know what to stand for. It is also important for them to learn that choosing friends with similar values will make peer pressure work *for* them instead of *against* them.

CREATIVE DEMONSTRATION

Make the following points with this demonstration:

- *Peer pressure can work for you or against you.*
- *It is difficult to stand alone for abstinence.*

Use a rope to demonstrate how peer pressure can be positive when you choose friends with high standards.

Ask friends or siblings to help with this demonstration. Use a piece of masking tape on the floor to represent a line or standard. Place one child on one side of the line and two or three on the other side. Using a short piece of rope, begin a tug of war between both sides. This demonstration will show how difficult it is to stand alone and hold on to a standard. Explain how peer pressure can work for you if you choose friends with similar values. You can make this fun by elaborating with realistic stories or situations.

LET'S THINK ABOUT IT...

"If you don't stand for something, you'll fall for anything."

CREATIVE DEMONSTRATION

Make the following points with this demonstration:

- *Friends will influence you positively or negatively.*
- *It's difficult to influence others when you are trying to stand alone.*

This demonstration will also illustrate the importance of having friends with similar values and standards. Prepare five clear plastic cups as follows:

1. *Your child's name — 1/2 cup water*
2. *"G" name — one drop of green food coloring*
3. *"R" name — one drop of red food coloring*
4. *"B" name — one drop of blue food coloring*
5. *"A" name — 1/4 cup bleach*

Use a boy/girl name that corresponds with the letter to help you remember the characters.

Tell a story where you use the cups to represent each character:

- Your child is committed to abstinence before marriage
- "G" is a follower who tries anything that his peers do to feel accepted, "green with envy"
- "R" is a lot of laughs, out for a good time, doesn't think about consequences, is sexually active, the "red hot lover"
- "B" doesn't have strong opinions about anything, doesn't like to make decisions, is moody and wishy-washy, "blah blue"
- "A" is a clear thinker, goal oriented, motivated, committed to abstinence before marriage

Fill each cup with 1/4 cup of water as you describe their personalities. Set the "A" cup aside. Using your child's cup, pour a little water into each of the remaining cups as you ask the question, *"How much do you think you can influence your friends who do not share your abstinence values?"* As you pour the clear water from your child's cup into the colored water cups, it shows that the clear water has very little effect. Next, pour a little water from each colored water cup into your child's cup. *"How much do you think your friends will influence you?"*

This demonstration shows the reality of having friends who do not share your values and standards. The more time and interaction you have with them, the more you will be influenced by them. It takes the support of friends to maintain strong moral values.

Now, take the "A" cup and begin mixing it with your child's cup. Pour the water back and forth representing the positive interaction between friends who have similar values and standards. Your child's thinking will begin to clear up (the bleach clears up the discolored water) and once again will be committed to abstinence values. It is very difficult to stand alone in a decision for abstinence. It is like swimming upstream in today's society and having a friend by your side is essential. Sometimes Christian friends will disappoint our children. It is not always guaranteed that they will have committed abstinence values. Just because someone claims to be a Christian does not necessarily mean they are choosing to follow God's standards.

Let's Think About It...

"As I associate, so I become."

Scriptures to Consider

Proverbs 13:20, I Corinthians 15:33, II Corinthians 6:14

SPIRITUAL MATURITY

Spiritual maturity means to grow in the knowledge and understanding of God. Just as a plant needs food, air, and water to grow, we need the Word, the Holy Spirit, prayer, fellowship and accountability with the Body of Christ to mature in Him. Because our spirituality encompasses every aspect of our lives, spiritual maturity will help us to develop emotional, mental, and social maturity as well. It will also give us self-discipline to keep our bodies as physically healthy as possible.

Scriptures to Consider

Colossians 1:10, II Peter 3:18, Hebrews 6:1, John 16:13

IN SUMMARY

Growing up is a lifetime process that involves a lot of hard work. Physical maturity is somewhat automatic, but adolescents experience different timetables and different rates of growth. Mental maturity requires a decision-making process that includes delaying immediate gratification and considering the consequences of choices. Goal setting/planning and setting limits of physical affection are also important aspects of mental maturity. Emotional maturity includes the practice of self-control and learning to handle our feelings in a healthy, respectful manner. Finally, spiritual maturity, growing in the knowledge and understanding of God, gives us the ability to mature in all areas of our lives.

Because peer pressure is the #1 reason teens become involved sexually before marriage, developing social maturity is extremely important. Children need to be taught that behavioral standards of right and wrong protect them from difficult consequences. Teach and model your moral standards and values with loving determination. Be patient and explain to them why you believe in God's absolute standards. Society is not shy about communicating its values to our children. Role-play challenging situations to help teens stand up for established standards. Encourage them to choose friends who have similar moral values and who can provide positive peer support.

Striving toward whole-person maturity is a process that enables our children to resist the pressures of premarital sex and maintain an abstinence goal. It is necessary to teach maturity by our example and our encouragement—recognizing and affirming each small step our children take towards becoming godly, responsible, caring adults.

Chapter 5

"Freedom!"

Whole-Person Benefits

As human beings, we value our freedom. It seems that sometimes we have to lose some of our freedom to really appreciate what we have. The sexual revolution of the '60s and '70s promoted *free sex*. However, this kind of sex actually carries a large price tag (as we have already examined in a previous chapter). Freedom does not come without its own price. Some of our forefathers and war veterans paid the ultimate price, their lives, for us to enjoy the freedoms we have today. Jesus Christ paid the ultimate price—His life—to give us freedom from the enslavement of our sin nature and to give us eternal life.

There is also a *cost, a price to pay,* to enjoy the benefits of sexual abstinence before marriage. It will cost teens in terms of delaying gratification, enduring ridicule and going against the crowd. It may cost them the loss of a desired relationship or a friendship, resulting in loneliness. But, the whole-person benefits of premarital sexual abstinence make the *WAIT!* worth all the painstaking efforts.

Scriptures to Consider

John 8:32

PHYSICAL BENEFITS

The physical benefits of sexual abstinence are most obvious. The risks of unplanned pregnancy and sexually transmitted diseases are eliminated. Teens protect their physical health and avoid all of the difficult decisions, pain and humiliation of unplanned pregnancy and disease. There is no concern about whether a condom or birth control device will work. There is no concern about difficulties with future reproductive health because of an abortion, childbirth or disease. In addition, risk of numerous complications of STD infection including cancers, arthritis and liver disease are avoided. In this time of life-threatening STDs, such as AIDS, abstinence is a lifesaving decision!

Teens are free to proceed with their lives, enjoying good health, full of energy and life to pursue their activities, sports and just plain old carefree fun.

LET'S THINK ABOUT IT...

"Your choices, not chance determine your destiny."

MENTAL BENEFITS

Abstinence gives the mind freedom from some of the less visible consequences of premarital sex. Abstinence assures that the commitment level of a relationship is not based on sexual intimacy. When a dating relationship ends, a young person will not have lingering memories of sexual intimacy that can make it difficult to move on to new relationships. Abstinence gives teens the freedom to set, plan and pursue their goals without distractions and delays related to sexual involvement. It eliminates worry or anxiety that often accompanies teen sexual activity. Their minds are free to concentrate on academics, activities, sports, social calendars and teen things. Teens are able to place high value on themselves and their *gift of sexuality*. They are free to develop a strong sense of self-respect, which in turn increases their ability to make responsible decisions and grow in competence. Painful, vivid memories will not interfere with their future sexual relationship within marriage. Guilt, inability to trust and jealousy related to premarital affairs will not plague their marital bond. Abstinence preserves the mind for a future fantastic sexual relationship within a committed marriage.

Let's Think About It...

"Abstinence is a 'mind preserver'."

EMOTIONAL BENEFITS

Abstinence gives freedom from the complicated feelings associated with premarital sex. A teen dating relationship can be more carefree and far less serious when sex is not included in the relationship. Abstinence *lessens* the tendency to be possessive, jealous and fearful of losing the relationship. The likelihood of conflict related to strong feelings of insecurity is minimized. There is freedom for the relationship to grow in more positive, healthy ways.

Teens are free from the painful feelings of being *used* and controlled by others who are pursuing self-gratification instead of their well-being. Broken relationships bring emotional pain, but there will be less anger, hurt, resentment and embarrassment if the couple was sexually abstinent. Teens can feel good about themselves and learn to pursue emotionally healthy relationships.

LET'S THINK ABOUT IT...

"Self-control protects your heart."

SOCIAL BENEFITS

Abstinence enables teens to focus on developing healthy, positive relationships based upon mutual respect. When sex is included in a relationship, it often becomes the focus of the relationship. The abstinent relationship is free to mature in all other aspects—mentally, emotionally, socially and spiritually without the physical distraction of sexual involvement.

Developing self-discipline in the sexual area of life promotes self-discipline in other areas of life. Teens learn to handle negative peer pressure and gain the respect of others. The rejection of others because of an unplanned pregnancy, abortion, sexually transmitted disease or tainted sexual reputation is avoided. Abstinent teens enjoy relationships that are trustworthy, more meaningful, lasting and rewarding. Their relationship with their parents is built on trust, which in turn creates a stronger parent/child bond and less conflict in the home. Since healthy, loving relationships are fundamental to a fulfilled life, concentrating on building relationships rather than physical pleasure brings long term benefits.

Let's Think About It…

"Show me your friends, I'll show you your future."

SPIRITUAL BENEFITS

The spiritual benefits of sexual purity allow us to experience God's best for our sexual lives. The marriage bed is pure and honorable. Our sexual expression is free to be all God designed it to be. We experience God's peace and are free of guilt and condemnation. We are free to pursue God and grow in Him. As a result, God will allow us to join Him in His redemptive work on earth—the ultimate privilege in this life!

Scriptures to Consider

Hebrews 13:4

IN SUMMARY

Sexual abstinence brings many freedoms and promotes healthy relationships. The overall health of our teens is greatly enhanced by premarital sexual abstinence. Their physical bodies are healthier, free of premature pregnancy and devastating sexually transmitted diseases. Their minds are free to concentrate on life as a teenager and are free from painful memories and lost dreams. Their emotional health is protected from the painful feelings that often accompany premarital sex and broken relationships. Their social lives are spontaneous and unhindered by complications of sexual involvement. Their spiritual lives are anchored by a commitment to God's standard of beliefs and values. They are free from guilt and condemnation and their relationship with God is unhindered. Teens are free to be teens—to have fun, to grow up and to learn how to love without having to face adult problems associated with premarital sex.

without your permission. Monitor the time your child spends on the Internet.

On the following page is an assignment for teens to evaluate the programs they watch. This work sheet can be used with all types of media. Discuss the results and reward them for a job well done. You may hear some complaints about the homework, but they will begin to learn to question the messages of the media.

TELEVISION: WHAT ARE YOU REALLY WATCHING?

Name a show you watch:______________________________________

1 What is the overall idea of the show? (i.e. single friends and their lives together, a married couple with a family, etc.)

____

____

____

____

2. How many different times do you see a couple in bed, or the suggestion of sexual activities? ________

3. How often do people talk about having had sex or how often do they hint in other ways they have had sex? (wearing bathrobes together in the morning, passionately kissing and then going into a room and shutting the door) ________

4. Is the couple married, dating or just friends, and what are their approximate ages?

❑ MARRIED ❑ DATING ❑ FRIENDS

AGES: M _____ F _____

5. Are sexually transmitted diseases (STDs) or pregnancy ever discussed as consequences? ❑ YES ❑ NO

6. Are there any mental, emotional, social or spiritual consequences shown on the program? ❑ YES ❑ NO

If YES, what are they? ______________________________________

____

____

7. Do you think that the sexual relationships shown on TV and movies reflect positive, committed relationships or God's standards?______________________________________

____

____

DATING

Keep your discussion about dating lighthearted. Share some of your dating experiences, including some of your worst dates and your best dates. If you had a date with a sexually aggressive person, share how you handled the situation and don't be afraid to be open with some of the mistakes you made in dating. Have some fun with this section.

What is the purpose of dating? Ask your child to share his/her ideas. Some responses might be:

- *Have a good time with someone you'd like to be with.*
- *Get to know ourselves and others better.*
- *Learn how to communicate with each other.*
- *Learn to be responsible and to respect others.*
- *Choose a marriage partner more wisely.*

LET'S TALK ABOUT IT...

Use the following questions to help with your discussion about dating.

When do you think a person should be allowed to date?
[maturity, trust and respect issues must be considered]

Are there any risks with starting to date too young?
[Studies show the younger dating begins, the greater the risk of sexual involvement.]

Are there any advantages of group dating over single dating? What are they?
[less pressure, more fun, not being alone and getting bored]

Why is it important to plan your dates?
[less opportunity for boredom and sexual involvement, use of drugs or alcohol]

Is it important to date only Christian teens or others with similar moral values? Why?
[eliminates pressure to compromise moral standards]

Be careful because some teens who call themselves Christians may not have high moral standards. Discuss the implications of II Corinthians 6:14.

Is it necessary to communicate your abstinence position early in a dating relationship? Why?
[keeps the pressure off of both, avoids one person pressuring the other, avoids misunderstandings]

What are some situations to avoid with a date?
[home alone, unchaperoned parties, drugs, alcohol]

Drugs and alcohol <u>increase</u> our desire for pleasure and <u>decrease</u> our ability to think clearly and make good judgments.

What are some fun things to do on a date?

As you explore some dating ideas, refer back to pages 92-95, *"drawing a line of affection."*

When each dating idea is shared, ask the question:

- ***Can you hold hands on this date?***
- ***Can you hug on this date?***
- ***Can you kiss on this date?***
- ***Can you get into the "underwear zone" on this date?***
- ***Can you have sexual intercourse on this date?***

To maintain an abstinence goal, it is important to plan dates so that they can be fun and safe. Avoiding situations where it would be easy to get involved sexually is a must. One of the most popular ideas for dates is going to a movie. Discuss why it is important to be careful of the movie selection. Watching a movie that has sexual scenes can tantalize the hormones and make abstinence difficult. Be honest and realistic about how our bodies respond to sexual media.

Let's Think About It...

"Don't let a hot date turn into a due date."

On the following page is a list of creative ideas for dates. Keep them handy when your teen begins the dating scene. Often, they are looking for suggestions. Ask your child for ideas to add to the list.

SUGGESTED CREATIVE IDEAS FOR A DATE

1. Play some game or sport together.
   Games: Monopoly, Pictionary, Ping Pong, Miniature Golf, Trivial Pursuit, Video Games, Put a Puzzle Together, Charades
   Sports: Tennis, Racquetball, Bowling, Golf, Bicycling, Roller or Ice Skating, Swimming, Skiing
2. Shop for and cook a meal together (fajitas, fondue, cookout, picnic, etc.).
3. Do things together such as washing the car, giving the dog a bath, etc.
4. Work out together (jog, bike, do aerobics, go to an exercise room).
5. Dinner Date: Try a different culture each week (Japanese, Mexican, Italian food restaurants).
6. Visit a park or zoo. Ride the city transit.
7. Go out for breakfast.
8. Go window shopping.
9. Videotape part of a double date. Go watch it together.
10. Read a book together.
11. Study.
12. Look at Christmas lights. Decorate a Christmas tree.
13. Do crafts or woodworking projects.
14. Bake cookies or brownies together (take them to a sick friend).
15. Plan and throw a party together.
16. Go to the fair, amusement park, flea market, craft show or rodeo.
17. Do some housework or mow a lawn for an elderly or disabled couple. Rake leaves and play in the pile of leaves.
18. Go shopping for each other: Go to a mall, set a $5-10 limit, separate and buy gifts to surprise each other.
19. Take a walk through the neighborhood.
20. Find some underprivileged children, orphans, or the kids next door and take them on an outing.
21. Have scavenger hunts. Involve other couples. (photo and audio scavenger hunts).
22. Have progressive dinners with friends.
23. Unit Dating—Two people ask two others for a date. No one is paired up.
24. Have a gourmet dinner party (read the cookbook and learn).
25. Use a video camera and stage your own game show or skit.
26. Have a costume theme party for the nearest holiday.

The following page includes comments collected from teens about how they like to be treated in a dating relationship. They are applicable to guys and girls. Use them as a discussion tool and then make a copy of them for your teen to refer to when they begin the dating process. Ask them if they agree with the statements and if they have additional thoughts to add to the list.

HEY GUY OR GIRL!

I'm attracted to attractiveness. *That involves more than good looks—it includes positive qualities like sensitivity, honesty and unselfishness. Personality, character and inner qualities make up for less than perfect looks.*

I'd like for you to have a good sense of humor. *I like it when you're fun to be with and you know how to laugh in all of life's hassles.*

I need you to respect my intelligence. *I like it when you ask my opinions about things and talk about ideas with me. Ask questions that will help me make up my own mind rather than tell me what to do.*

I need you to give me space. *I like it when you don't push me to tell you every detail. Know when to stop asking questions, and you don't have to know every place I've gone and with whom.*

I need to feel important to you. *I like it when you ask about my day and sometimes say "no" to other people and other activities so you can spend time with me. Please include me in the conversation when we're in a group.*

I need you to listen when I talk to you. *I like it when you stop what you're doing and look me in the eyes.*

I need you to be thoughtful. *I like it when you use decent manners and remember my birthday and other important dates for me.*

I need you to be sensitive. *I like it when you aren't afraid of tears (mine or yours). Please ask me what I'm feeling and what you can do for me. Be willing to accept silence sometimes.*

I need you to be supportive. *I like it when you compliment me, attend my activities and learn about something that interests me. Please be excited when I try something new.*

I need you to believe in me. *I like it when you don't put me down for my mistakes and say, "that was a stupid thing to do." Tell me it's OK even when I can't explain myself to you. Sometimes I don't understand myself either.*

I need you to be loyal to me. *I like it when you keep your word. When you say you will do something, you do it. When you say you will be there, you're there. Know when to keep quiet about a confidence I've shared with you. (The feeling of betrayal is deadly.)*

I need you to respect my body. *I like it when you don't make cheap jokes about it. Don't act as though you have "exploration rights" to it. Don't pressure me to hand over my virginity before marriage.*

LOVE AND COMMITMENT

Just as a love relationship is not possible without respect, an authentic love relationship requires commitment.

What is the definition of commitment?
[sticking with a promise or responsibility, refusing to quit regardless of the circumstances]

Ask your child to give you some examples of commitment in his/her life right now.
[commitment to Christ, a sport, studies, a job, family, etc.]

Commitment is a learned behavior and requires some level of maturity. Your example of your commitment to Christ and commitment in your relationships will speak louder than anything you can say. Perhaps you can share about some of the difficult times you have had in relationships and how your level of commitment has preserved those relationships.

LET'S TAKE A CLOSER LOOK...

Draw a simple house structure to compare building a healthy relationship with building a house. The foundation of a healthy relationship is *friendship.*

Discuss some of the qualities of a true friend.
[respectful, sensitive, good listener, loyal, committed, caring, accepting, forgiving, has similar interests and values]

The word friendship comes from the Indo-European word "prei," which means "FREE." Each person must be *free* to be themselves. True friendship is a give and take relationship and is not one-sided. Friendship takes effort, commitment and maintenance. Encourage your teens to concentrate on building friendships in their dating relationships. If they keep a commitment to sexual abstinence, they will be able to concentrate on the relational aspect, instead of gravitating to the physical side of their relationship. When a break-up occurs, they will experience a loss but will have far less painful consequences. The spiritual foundation for a healthy relationship is Jesus Christ. (See I Corinthians 3:11) This spiritual foundation will keep each partner strong and committed to God's plan for life and relationships.

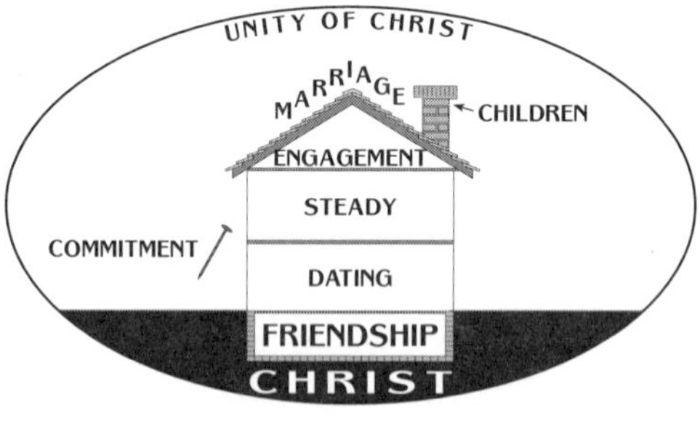

How important is a foundation to a house?
[very important]

What is the purpose of a foundation? Just as a house needs a good foundation to stand the test of time and to weather the storms, healthy relationships need the spiritual foundation of Jesus Christ and the relational foundation of friendship. If the dating relationship progresses, along with friendship, love and commitment, the couple may desire engagement and marriage. The best marriages continue to nurture marital friendship, along with their relationship with Christ.

Relationships need *commitment* to stay together for the long haul. *Commitment* can be compared to the nails that are used to hold a house together. The house will not stay together without nails. A relationship will not stay together without *commitment*. Occasionally, the house will need some maintenance (inside and out), just as marriage relationships need work and maintenance. The overall bond that holds a marriage relationship together is the unity of Christ.

Discuss some examples of the storms that may test the strength and commitment of a relationship (health, financial, family problems). These problems are inevitable. Our foundation in Christ, friendship and commitment will enable our marriage to stand firm and not crumble when the storms rage. (See Matthew 7:24-27.)

When is the best time to include children in a relationship?
[after marriage]

Premarital sex can obviously produce children before marriage. The complications of this are discussed in Chapter 3.

AFFECTION AND COMMITMENT

Affection and commitment must be balanced in a relationship.

What is the fullest amount of <u>physical affection</u> in a relationship?
[sexual intercourse]

How can we judge how much <u>physical affection</u> is appropriate in a relationship?

What is the fullest amount of <u>commitment</u> in a relationship?
[marriage]

What makes marriage more of a <u>commitment</u> than living together?
[Marriage involves inviting friends to witness; making promises publicly before God and an authority figure; a religious ceremony, rings as symbols of the commitment, etc. Living together gives the connotation that the door is cracked open, just in case the relationship doesn't work.]

Draw a divided heart to illustrate the importance of both sides of the heart. (*Physical affection & commitment* should be equally balanced.)

The amount of *physical affection* in a relationship should equal the *commitment* in a relationship. This gives the best opportunity for the relationship to stay together and avoid a broken heart.

Many relationships that we see today are out of balance. The amount of physical affection is much greater than the commitment in the relationship. These relationships will not last—they will eventually fall apart.

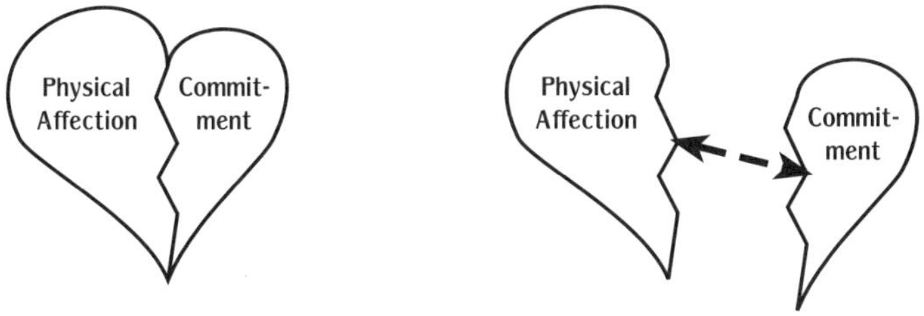

Review *"drawing a line of affection"* from Chapter 4. Using the heart illustration, determine where a dating relationship becomes out of balance.

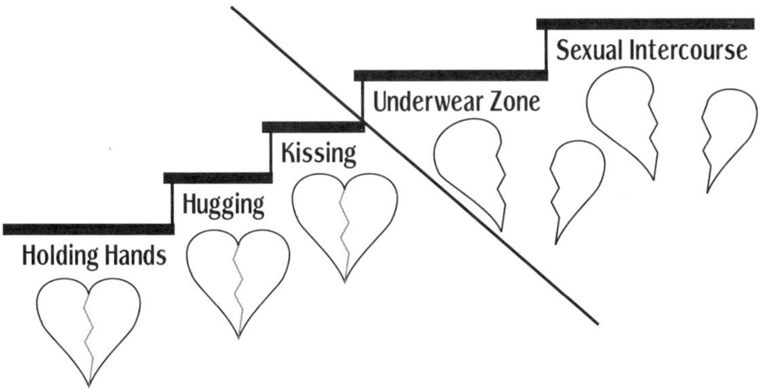

The amount of *physical affection* and *commitment* in a relationship must be equal for the relationship to be healthy and to have longevity. God's plan to save our gift of sexuality for marriage provides us with the best opportunity for a fulfilling relationship.

"Remember that your bodies are created with the same dignity as the body of Christ. In sexual sin we violate the sacredness of our own bodies, these bodies that were made for God-given and God-modeled love, for 'becoming one' with another." I Corinthians 6:18-20 (*The MESSAGE*)[33]

God-modeled Love

SECONDARY VIRGINITY

"I have already lost my virginity; but after taking this class, I plan to stop having sex and save myself for my future husband."

"My decision is secondary virginity. Not ever again will I have sex until my wedding night."

"I have already had a baby. I wish someone would have told me that I should wait to have sex until I get married."

These quotes are from junior high students who have taken our abstinence course and have changed their attitude with regard to premarital sex.

After suffering painful consequences, many teens are making a decision for secondary virginity.

Once teens become sexually active, is it possible for them to stop and start over?
[YES!]

What changes may have to take place in order for this to be accomplished?
(Ask your teen for some suggestions).

- *The decision needs to come from the heart. "I want to stop." This requires confession and repentance.*
- *If the partner involved in the sexual relationship does not have the same commitment, the relationship will have to end.*
- *Teens who want to stop need to have friends who are committed to abstinence. If their friends are sexually active, it's time to find some new friends.*
- *It is helpful to be accountable to someone for this decision and commitment. (another committed friend, a counselor, parent, pastor, youth worker or a trusted adult)*
- *Pursue new interests through sports, clubs, work, hobbies, volunteer work etc.*

- *With a parent, trusted adult friend or counselor, take a close look at the reasons behind the sexual involvement. Work through the emotional issues including guilt and shame. See Chapter 2.*
- *Avoid situations that could lead to sexual involvement, including time alone together, unchaperoned parties or the use of alcohol and drugs.*
- *Talk about your standards up front with a date and "draw a line of affection" at kissing or less.*

Even when teens have had a sexual relationship, it is never too late to stop their sexual activity and make a new beginning for their lives. There may still be consequences as a result of their choices, but they can begin to rebuild their self-worth and experience more healthy relationships by making an abstinence commitment. This will not be an easy decision to maintain, but there will be lasting benefits that will outweigh the difficulties. A life that is committed to Christ has the power to overcome temptations.

Scriptures to Consider

Proverbs 3:6, II Corinthians 5:17, 7:10-11, I John 1:9

GOD'S PLAN OR THE WORLD'S PLAN?

Life is full of choices. God has given us a free will to make those choices, which in turn, greatly impact our success in relationships and life. Sometimes we blame other people or circumstances for our failures.

Ultimately, we must bear the responsibility for our successes and our failures because we have the ability to choose how we will respond to even the most difficult people and painful circumstances in our lives.

Teens also have a choice as to how they will respond to the challenge of saving their *gift of sexuality* for a marriage relationship. *Is it worth the wait?* They will have to decide. After we have exhausted our efforts of teaching and modeling appropriate behaviors, they have the final say as to how they will respond. Parents cannot take the responsibility for the choices their children make.

GOD'S PLAN	This plan is to wait until marriage to become involved sexually with a person.
WORLD'S PLAN	This plan is **not** to wait until marriage for sexual involvement.

GOD'S PLAN is the *best* plan that offers healthy, lasting relationships, avoids painful consequences and gives the freedom to pursue personal goals and dreams.

THE WORLD'S PLAN is a *counterfeit* of the best plan for our lives that may result in painful consequences and the loss of personal goals and dreams.

Even when teens follow **THE WORLD'S PLAN**, at any time they can make a decision to return to **GOD'S PLAN**. There may be some consequences to endure, but there is always an opportunity with God's help to make a new beginning in their lives.

Scriptures to Consider

I Thessalonians 4:2-7

IN SUMMARY

There is a lot of confusion in today's society about love, sex, and relationships. Children need to be taught about the characteristics of authentic love, including respect and commitment. The media plays a powerful role in shaping the thoughts of mainstream society, including our children. Many voices are calling out to them to live for today and to forsake any absolute standards. Our young people need to learn to examine the underlying messages that daily bombard them. They do not have to act as helpless robots with no brains.

Our teens have the ability to choose what they want for their lives. Parents have the awesome responsibility to teach God's standards of right and wrong and to model healthy relationships. We must take the time to talk with them about dating relationships, setting limits of physical affection and appropriate behaviors. We must model true friendship, love and commitment.

Our teens need encouragement and hope when they experience failures. They need to understand God's love and forgiveness. Even if they have had sexual experiences, they can reevaluate their behavior and make a new beginning with secondary virginity. Because society no longer supports the value of right and wrong with regard to sexual issues, our children need the love and support of their parents, school, clubs, church, etc. to encourage them to stick with abstinence because it is *worth the wait!*

Let's Think About It...

"The best offense is a good defense."

Chapter 7

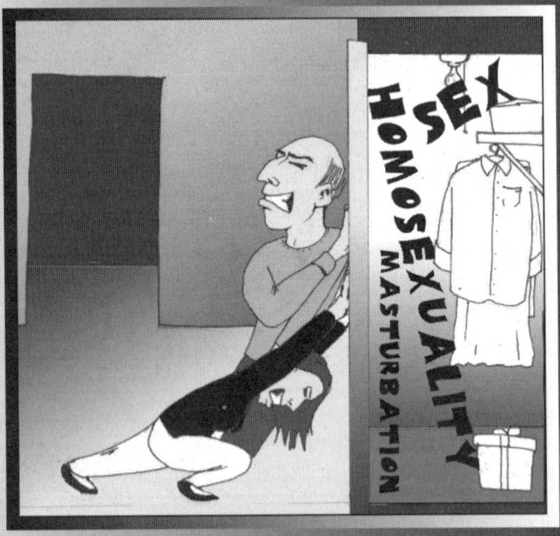

"We can't talk about that!"

Homosexuality, Masturbation, & Sexual Abuse

Some topics are more difficult to discuss with your children than others. The *Bible* clearly addresses the issue of homosexuality. The teaching about masturbation is less definitive. I will share some biblical guidelines that I developed after consulting with several pastors.

HOMOSEXUALITY

Homosexuality is defined as having sexual attraction to or sexual activity with members of one's own sex. The development of homosexuality is very complex. Several common factors may contribute to an individual being drawn to the homosexual lifestyle. Many homosexuals have a background of sexual abuse and/or dysfunctional relationships with the same sex parent. Research indicates that homosexuals often struggle with sexual addiction. Fifty-seven per cent of homosexuals report having had more than thirty partners over their lifetime and thirty-five per cent report more than one hundred.[34]

The controversy rages as to whether homosexuality is a genetic trait or learned behavior. Researchers have tried to link homosexuality with genetics, but their studies have been inconclusive. Our loving, just God would never create homosexuals, then emphatically forbid the fulfillment of their gift of sexuality. The *Bible* clearly describes the practice of homosexuality as unnatural and an abomination to God.

As parents, it is our responsibility to share our beliefs with our children and to be open to discussing their questions. Some of their questions may be with regard to sexual terms or acts they have heard from peers or through the media. An honest response of "I don't know" is always appropriate, but be open to finding answers to your child's questions. Because homosexuality has become a political issue, there are many underlying messages relayed through the media.

Teaching your teen to recognize media bias is very important (as previously discussed). Look at scriptures together. Talking openly about the foundation of your beliefs will help your teen to more accurately evaluate the issue.

Because homosexuality has emerged to the forefront of controversial issues today, children are forced to evaluate their beliefs when they are young and most vulnerable in their development process. This can cause some children to become fearful that they are homosexual when they experience strong feelings for another child of the same sex. They need our reassurance that these feelings are normal and that nonsexual physical affection is very appropriate in same sex relationships and is not an indication of homosexuality. Some young people who have been approached or abused by a homosexual may begin to question their sexual identity and can experience anger in addition to fear and confusion. The confusion and anger can be intense if their bodies responded to the suggestion of or an act of sexual stimulation. Sexual identity can invoke deep emotional issues that underline the importance of your availability to talk through these sexual issues with your child. If your child is struggling with sexual identity issues and you feel inadequate to address them, do not hesitate to seek assistance from clergy and/or professional counselors.

Homosexuals deserve to be treated with respect and love. We are called to love one another, but to hate sin. Romans 3:23 reminds us that we all have sinned and fallen short of the glory of God. God calls us to confession and repentance. There's a pharisee in most of us that wants to judge and shun the homosexual. Instead, we are called to love homosexuals and lead them to the healing touch of Christ. Your children will most likely adopt your attitudes. Carefully explain your belief system to your child and model respect for all of humanity. At some point, our children will establish their own belief system based upon our parental influence, God's work in their lives, their experiences and their choices.

Scriptures to Consider

Leviticus 18:22, 20:13; Romans 1:26-27, I Corinthians 6:9-10

MASTURBATION

Masturbation is the stimulation of the genital organs to orgasm achieved by manual or other bodily contact, exclusive of sexual intercourse. Some common reasons for masturbation are for self-discovery, for pleasure, to relieve sexual tension, to alleviate loneliness, to relax for sleep, or simply because it has become a habit. Masturbation is a moral issue on which even the most conservative Christians do not agree. It is fairly common among adolescents. A child may or may not feel a need to masturbate. If masturbation becomes excessive, there may be an indication of an emotional or spiritual problem. Feelings of guilt connected with masturbation can cause mental, emotional or spiritual anguish.

The *Bible* does not specifically address the act of masturbation, but it is very clear about how we should love God, ourselves and others. When is masturbation a sin?

Perhaps we can answer this question by looking at the suggested scriptures:

Masturbation is obviously sinful when it involves the following:

- *lust (immoral thoughts)—Matthew 5:27-28, Romans 6:12-14, 12:1, 13:14, James 1:14-15, I Peter 2:11, I John 2:16*
- *dehumanizing others—Philippians 2:3*
- *becoming an uncontrollable habit—I Corinthians 6:12-13*
- *guilt, shame, self-hatred*
- *fantasy—Philippians 4:8*

One young man who felt controlled by masturbation said he found the following actions helpful in conquering his habit:

- *Write down reasons why you don't want to do it and why you don't have to do it. Memorize scriptures and use them to renew your mind.*
- *When tempted to masturbate, read the list and scriptures and realize that Christ gives you the power to overcome the temptation. (See I Corinthians 10:13 and Philippians 4:13.)*

- *Try to anticipate when you may be tempted, and decide ahead of time you will not do it. (See Psalm 119:9-11.)*
- *Be accountable to a friend who supports your decision to stop. (See James 5:16.)*

It is recommended that, if possible, fathers or other trusted adult males talk to their sons about masturbation, while mothers or other trusted adult females talk to their daughters.

SEXUAL ABUSE

Sexual abuse includes the seduction and commitment of a sexual act with a child or reluctant adult. This may include touching, exposure or forcing the victim to touch the perpetrator or expose themselves. Where is the line drawn between sexual abuse and sexual harassment? Certainly physical acts constitute abuse. However, sexual antics, lewd language and exposure to pornographic materials labeled by some as harassment, would be defined as abuse by others. Regardless of whether we label it as abuse or harassment, sexual abuse is a major assault on human dignity. Dr. Dan Allender in his book, *The Wounded Heart* explains the profound effect of sexual abuse and describes the factors that shape our dignity as:

- *The ability to have relationships—with God and others.*
- *The desire to have significance—to be competent, in control*

Sexual abuse distorts our relationship with God and others. It has a profound effect on our self-worth and creates a sense of powerlessness. Those who are abused struggle with extreme issues of shame. This is why it is so important to emphasize that the abuse was not their fault. The shame that they experience is illegitimate shame. Illegitimate shame exposes some element of our dignity and leads to self-contempt/other-centered contempt which leads to sorrow and death. Illegitimate shame is Satan's counterfeit of biblical humbling. It is too intense and self-absorbed to be from God. Legitimate shame exposes our sin. It is biblical humbling and leads to repentance and life. "A godly response in the face of abuse is to grieve—for the perpetrator's sin and for the damage done to our soul."[35] Healing occurs when we become reconciled to the issue and mankind, not necessarily to the abuser. Forgiveness says, "I have scars of the abuse. I'm not saying that it doesn't hurt, but I accept that I must live with the consequences of being abused. I will suffer the consequences, regardless. Therefore, forgiveness and healing will only come when I am willing to let go of the desire for revenge, let go of my bitterness and hatred. I must be willing to let God judge and deal with my abuser." It is essential that those who have been victimized by abuse or harassment receive counseling and support. Sexual abuse by a family member injures the soul of the family. In all situations of sexual abuse, family counseling is recommended.

By law, sexual abuse must be reported to the proper authorities. Some parents may be reluctant to report abuse for various reasons. Keep in mind that if your child has been abused or harassed, it is likely that the perpetrator is preying upon others. The only way to begin the process of stopping the abuser is by reporting it to the authorities.

Be cautious about allowing your child to spend the night with friends. Since this is a very popular thing to do, it is sometimes difficult to say no. Being acquainted with the family is not always an indication of safety. Try to find the balance between good judgment and paranoia. Teach your children that if they are feeling uneasy about anyone in the home, they should call you and, if necessary, make up an excuse to come home.

DATE RAPE is becoming far too prevalent. According to a study in 1994, 74 percent of girls who had sex before the age of 14 and 60 percent who had sex before the age of 15 described their first sexual experience as rape.[36] More than 15 percent of college women have been raped since they turned eighteen. Thirty-two percent of all rapes occur when the victim is between the ages of eleven and seventeen.[37] Talk with your teen about how to avoid date rape. It can happen to anyone. Review the information on dating in Chapter 6. Explore possible escape plans, such as screaming, kicking in the groin, biting, poking in the eyes—whatever it takes to break free of a perpetrator. Enrolling daughters in a self-defense class is a good investment. Tell your children that you'll pick them up anywhere, anytime, no questions asked. Give your teen a mobile phone or plenty of quarters so that you are just a phone call away. Emphasize that they should not accept rides with someone they just met or think they know pretty well. They must not be in a house alone with their date. They must avoid the alcohol/drug scene. Numerous rapes occur at parties. This is a very frightening topic for parents—we must warn our teens of all possibilities. No one has a right to take advantage of them. Anytime a person says "NO" and the perpetrator continues, it is RAPE!

DATING VIOLENCE affects 28 percent of teenagers in an intimate relationship, according to the Family Research Laboratory at the University of New Hampshire. Alcohol and drug use make already volatile situations worse. Some teens grow up in families where violence and abuse is the norm. They start dating and either become the abuser or the victim. Victims are afraid to tell their parents or friends because they don't want to appear stupid for tolerating abuse or feeling too weak to end an abusive relationship. The following list is a self-test given by the Nebraska Domestic Violence and Sexual Assault Coalition to help identify signs of an abusive relationship. **Share the self-test on the following page with your teen.**

Does your boyfriend/girlfriend ...

- Isolate you from people you care about most or from friends you had before you began dating?
- Frequently embarrass or make fun of you in front of other people?
- Use intimidation to make you do what he/she wants?
- Make you feel there is "no way out" of the relationship?
- Make you perform sexual acts that you don't enjoy?
- Threaten you with force, words or weapons?
- Use alcohol or drugs as an excuse for saying hurtful things or abusing you?
- Get extremely angry frequently and you don't understand why?
- Not believe he/she has hurt you or blame you for what has happened?
- Physically force you to do what you do not want to do?

Other signs are: not seeing you as an equal, getting unreasonably frustrated if you don't go along with his/her ideas or showing cruelty to people, animals or children.

If you suspect your teen is involved in an abusive relationship, try to stay calm and get some professional counsel and support for your child and yourself.

IN SUMMARY

Even though the topics of homosexuality, masturbation and sexual abuse are more difficult to discuss with your child, do not procrastinate. The topics of homosexuality and masturbation must be explained with a biblical foundation and your personal convictions. Be careful to avoid lecturing your teen. Instead, share the *Word*, along with how you have reached your convictions with regard to these issues. Good communication is a two-way conversation. Allow your children to express their viewpoints and respect their opinions, even if you disagree with them. Often, as adolescents, they may choose to oppose our viewpoints just to show autonomy. With time and maturity, they will eventually form their own beliefs and convictions.

Sexual abuse, date rape and dating violence are rampant in today's society. Talk with your children about ways to avoid becoming a victim. Teach them to become cautious in their relationships without paranoia. The possibility of our children becoming a victim of one of these crimes is very unnerving. We must prepare them as best we can, realizing that at times these situations can occur even when all precautions have been taken. A victim should never be made to feel responsible for abuse they have suffered. Victims and their families will need biblical counseling and support.

These discussions could save your teenager from painful consequences. Taking the time to discuss these important issues shows teens how much you love them. They may complain about having these talks, but deep down inside, they know that it's because you care and for that, they are thankful.

"It's not as hard as we thought!"

Never Give Up!

Our young people today are under tremendous pressure to become involved sexually before marriage. The supportive restraints that were once available through society just one generation ago are no longer available. The devastating effects of the sexual revolution and the destruction of moral absolutes have lured this generation of teens into sexual chaos. Our adolescents are facing sexual pressure at a younger age than previous generations because of the earlier onset of puberty and the mass media sexual campaign. Dr. Lloyd Kolbe, the Director of the Centers for Disease Control's Division of Adolescent and School Health, said, "It's going to take a sophisticated, large-scale effort, uniting families, schools, religious groups, health agencies, and community groups, to discourage teens from having sex."[38] Research indicates that parents who communicate with their children about sexuality, offering guidance and supervision, greatly reduce the risk of their children experimenting with premarital sex. Our children deserve and desperately need our help. They need God's power within themselves to resist the ongoing temptation of sexual sin.

Many young people today feel hopeless about the future as indicated by the rising suicide rate among teens. This hopelessness also propels the need to escape through drugs, alcohol and sexual activity. Seeking immediate gratification is encouraged and applauded by our morally anemic society. Where are the moral heroes of today? Government leaders, famous sports figures, even many so called "men of God" have slid down the slippery slope of moral decadence. It's no wonder that many teens fall prey to the path of *escape*.

What are we to do? As parents, is it time to throw in the towel? ABSOLUTELY NOT! Our children are worth fighting for! We must be more diligent to teach them the truth, model moral character and love them generously. We must provide them with God's standards to live by and nurturing relationships within the family. We must earnestly seek God's help to enter this battlefield we call life and give parenting our very best shot.

General Anatomy Information

PUBERTY

Puberty is the stage of life at which a child turns into a young man or young woman, when the reproductive organs become functional and secondary sex characteristics develop. Adolescence is the period between puberty and adulthood (the end of body growth). Boys and girls experience different rates of growth, with boys lagging about two years behind girls. The pituitary gland is the "time clock" that determines when the growth process begins. It is located at the base of the brain and sets off the signal that sends out hormones to cause the reproductive organs to begin development.

Changes that take place in the physical body are:

Girls: body hair, breast development, hips broaden, waist narrows, reproductive organs further develop

Boys: body hair, shoulders broaden, muscle mass and bone length increase, hips narrow, voice deepens, reproductive organs further develop

Other changes that take place involve the skin and perspiration. New sweat glands produce perspiration when you are nervous or afraid. Skin becomes more oily and thickens so that pores become plugged and pimples develop.

Adolescent and teen girls may experience more mood swings, crying spells and feelings of agitation that are related to the fluctuation of hormones within their bodies. Menstruation can bring a number of side-effects, including headaches, backaches, cramps, nausea and water retention. Many girls experience swelling and tenderness in their breasts just before their period arrives. They are often concerned about the size of their breasts and can become especially vulnerable to male reactions. They may need extra assurance during this time of their lives.

Adolescent and teen boys experience spontaneous erections frequently because of high or fluctuating levels of testosterone. They also experience nocturnal emissions, involuntary orgasm and ejaculation of semen during sleep (wet dreams). An erection can be caused by having to urinate, being excited, experiencing sexual arousal or friction on the pants.

It is not unusual for one testicle to hang lower than the other. Sometimes the scrotum hangs loosely to keep the testicles cooler, and then at other times, the scrotum tightens close to the body to keep the sperm warm. This is the body's way of keeping the sperm the right temperature. The scrotum also tightens when a male is frightened.

FEMALE BODY'S ROLE IN REPRODUCTION

Thousands of eggs (or ovum) are present in the girl's body. The ovaries are the two internal sex organs that produce the eggs and the female sex hormones. Somewhere near mid-cycle, ovulation takes place. The fallopian tube brushes against the ovary follicle, causing the egg to be released from the ovary. The egg is the size of a grain of sand and is drawn through the tube by muscle contractions that move it toward the uterus. The journey down this 5" tube takes 3-4 days and the egg must be fertilized within 18-24 hours. After sexual intercourse, if a sperm fertilizes the egg, it makes its way to the uterus, where it embeds in the lining. The walls of the uterus have thickened to prepare for the fertilized egg. The blood supply increases to the uterus, and if fertilization does not take place, the extra lining and blood discharge from the body. This is called menstruation. Menstruation can be quite irregular for the first two or three years. Later, a cycle of 3-5 weeks is normal.

MALE BODY'S ROLE IN REPRODUCTION

Each testicle is packed with tubes and the walls of tubes are lined with special cells. During adolescence, the cells develop into sperm. Approximately 100 million are produced every 24 hours. After the sperm are produced in the testes, they move to the epididymis to mature (for about six weeks). They then move through the vas deferens and are stored in the seminal vesicles until ejaculation. Semen consists mostly of the fluids from the Cowper's and prostate glands in addition to the sperm.

The fluid that is released before ejaculation contains sperm, and therefore could impregnate a girl. There are 400-500 million sperm per ejaculation—20 percent of these are defective and only about 50 finally reach the egg. (About one-half teaspoon of fluid is ejaculated). It takes about 40 minutes for sperm to migrate from the cervix through the uterus and up to the outer fallopian tubes. Sperm can survive up to three days inside the woman's body.

In preparation for the passing of sperm, the penis becomes congested with blood and becomes erect. Muscular contractions force the semen into the urethra and out of the body. During sexual intercourse, the sperm propel themselves into the vagina, through the cervix and into the fallopian tubes. It is quite possible for sperm just outside the vagina to swim inside. If there is sperm in the fallopian tube when an ovum is released, the sperm can fertilize it. Once a sperm penetrates an egg, the egg is sealed from any other sperm penetration. After an egg is fertilized in the next few days, one cell becomes 2, then 4, 8, then 16. After one week (while still dividing), it reaches the uterus and embeds in the soft lining where growth continues.

TWINS

Identical—one egg is fertilized by one sperm, but the egg divides into two separate babies that are genetically identical with the same biological make-up

Fraternal—two eggs are fertilized by two separate sperm forming two biologically different babies—just like brothers and sisters

FEMALE REPRODUCTIVE SYSTEM

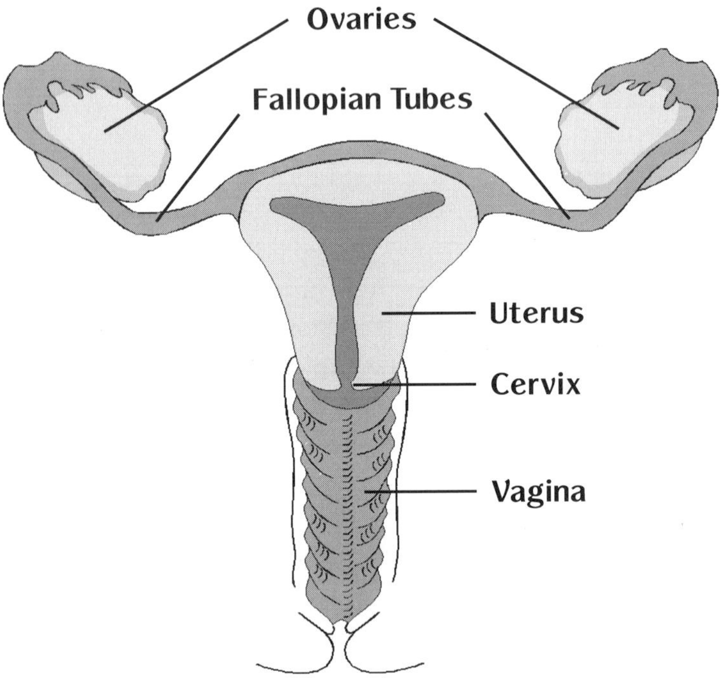

MALE REPRODUCTIVE SYSTEM

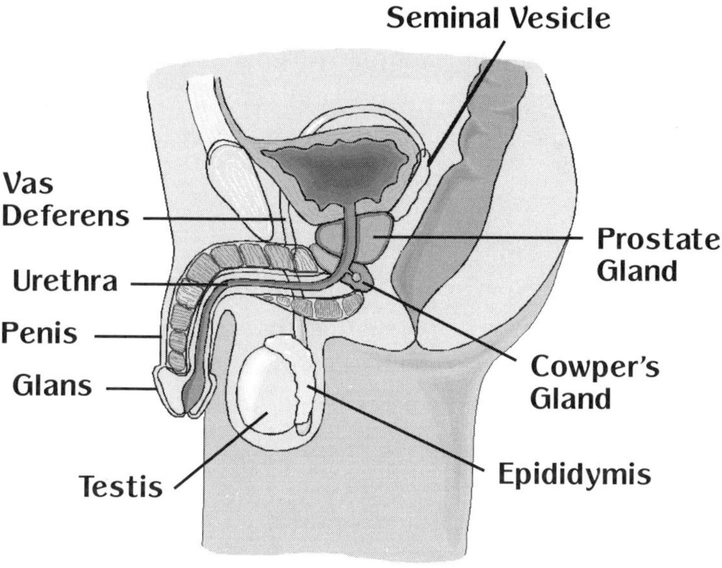

Fetal Development

The following information is provided to help you answer questions about fetal development. The growth pattern described is recognized medical information, documented by scientific research. Slight variations in developmental days may exist from individual to individual.

THE FIRST NINE MONTHS

DAY 1	Sperm joins with ovum (egg) to form one cell—smaller than a grain of salt. The new life has inherited 23 chromosomes from each parent, 46 in all. This one cell contains the complex genetic blueprint for every detail of human development—the child's sex, hair and eye color, height, skin tone.
DAYS 3-4	The fertilized egg travels down the fallopian tube into the uterus, where the lining has been prepared for implantation.
DAYS 5-9	During this time, the fertilized egg implants itself in the rich lining of the uterus and begins to draw nourishment.

DAYS 10-14	The developing embryo signals its presence through placental chemicals and hormones, preventing the mother from menstruating.
DAY 20	Foundations of the brain, spinal cord and nervous system are already established.
DAY 21	The heart begins to beat.
DAY 28	The backbone and muscles are forming. Arms, legs, eyes and ears have begun to show.
DAY 30	At one month old, the embryo is 10,000 times larger than the original fertilized egg—and developing rapidly. The heart is pumping increasing quantities of blood through the circulatory system. The placenta forms a unique barrier that keeps the mother's blood separate while allowing food and oxygen to pass through to the embryo.
DAY 35	Five fingers can be discerned in the hand. The eyes darken as pigment is produced.
DAY 40	Brain waves can be detected and recorded.
WEEK 6	The liver is now taking over the production of blood cells, and the brain begins to control movement of muscles and organs. The mother is about to miss her second period and has probably confirmed that she is pregnant.

WEEK 7	The embryo begins to move spontaneously. The jaw forms, including teeth buds in the gums. Soon the eyelids will seal to protect the embryo's developing light-sensitive eyes, and will reopen at about the seventh month.
WEEK 8	At a little more than an inch long, the developing life is now called a fetus—Latin for "young one" or "offspring." Everything is now present that will be found in a fully developed adult. The heart has been beating for more than a month, the stomach produces digestive juices and the kidneys have begun to function. Forty muscle sets begin to operate in conjunction with the nervous system. The fetus' body responds to touch, although the mother will not be able to feel movement until the fourth or fifth month.
WEEK 9	Fingerprints are already evident in the skin. The fetus will curve its fingers around an object placed in the palm of its hand.
WEEK 10	The uterus has now doubled in size. The fetus can squint, swallow and wrinkle its forehead.
WEEK 11	At this time, the fetus is about two inches long. Urination occurs. The face has assumed a baby's profile, and muscle movements are becoming more coordinated.

WEEK 12	The fetus now sleeps, awakens and exercises its muscles energetically—turning its head, curling its toes, and opening and closing its mouth. The palm, when stroked, will make a tight fist. The fetus breathes amniotic fluid to help develop its respiratory system.
WEEK 13	Fine hair has begun to grow on the head, and sexual differentiation has become apparent.
MONTH 4	By the end of this month, the fetus is eight to ten inches in length and weighs a half pound or more. The mother will probably start to "show" now. The ears are functioning, and there is evidence that the fetus hears quite a bit: the mother's voice and heartbeat as well as external noises. The umbilical cord has become an engineering marvel, transporting 300 quarts of fluids per day and completing a round-trip of fluids every 30 seconds.
MONTH 5	Half the pregnancy has now passed, and the fetus is about 12 inches long. The mother has definitely begun to feel movement by now. If a sound is especially loud or startling, the fetus may jump in reaction to it.
MONTH 6	Oil and sweat glands are functioning. The delicate skin of the growing baby is protected from the fetal waters by a

special ointment called "vernix." If the baby were born in this month and given the proper care, he would survive.

MONTH 7 The baby now uses the four senses of vision, hearing, taste and touch. He can recognize his mother's voice.

MONTH 8 The skin begins to thicken, with a layer of fat stored underneath for insulation and nourishment. Antibodies increasingly build up. The baby absorbs a gallon of amniotic fluid per day; the fluid is completely replaced every three hours.

MONTH 9 Toward the end of this month, the baby is ready for birth. The average duration of pregnancy is 280 days from the first day of the mother's last menstrual period, but this varies. Most babies (85 percent to 95 percent) are born somewhere between 266 and 294 days. By this time the infant normally weighs six to nine pounds, and his heart is pumping 300 gallons of blood per day. He is fully capable of life outside the womb.

The First Nine Months. Copyright 1989, 1994, 1995, Focus on the Family. All rights reserved. International copyright secured. Used by permission.

NOTE: There are a number of videos available that show fetal development and the birth of a baby. Check with your local library or video store if you are interested.

The 10 Most Common STDs

AIDS (ACQUIRED IMMUNE DEFICIENCY SYNDROME)

What is it? Condition caused by Human Immunodeficiency Virus (HIV) that attacks and destroys body's immune system, leaving victim open to a variety of unusual life-threatening illnesses. Incubation period: 1-10 years. No vaccine, no cure. At greatest risk are those who have or have had other sexually transmitted diseases, drug users, homosexuals.

Transmission: By oral sex, anal sex or vaginal intercourse with someone infected by HIV (the AIDS virus). Spread by transfer of body fluids in sex, sharing dirty needles, contaminated blood. Infected woman may transmit AIDS through bloodstream to unborn child, through body fluids as child is born, or through breast-feeding. Not spread by casual contact. Virus found in blood, semen, other body fluids.

Symptoms: 1) Some have no immediate symptoms; may not get sick but are carriers. Some have illness like mononucleosis. 2) Victims develop antibodies to AIDS; no outward symptoms but are carriers. 3) AIDS-Related Condition—ARC: swollen lymph glands, night sweats, fever, diarrhea, weight loss, fatigue, possibly thrush and shingles. 4) AIDS — immune system destroyed. Victim gets fatal disease.

Potential Effects: Deadly. Not everyone infected with virus gets AIDS, but at least 75% of those in the U.S. estimated to carry AIDS virus with no symptoms now will develop full-blown, fatal AIDS in 5-7 years. (Some estimates are higher.)

Occurrence: Spreading. Positive blood test doesn't indicate fatal AIDS. It means exposure to HIV has occurred, the person has become a carrier and is at risk of having and/or spreading a fatal disease.

Treatment: NO CURE. New tests for early specific identification of HIV infection are now being released for help in diagnosis. New medications to help control, but not cure, AIDS are being introduced regularly. More are being tested around the world.

CHLAMYDIA (INCLUDING NON-GONOCOCCAL URETHRITIS (NGU) IN MEN)

What is it? Bacterial infection in urinary and reproductive organs. Can lead to NGU (Non-Gonococcal Urethritis) in men; PID (Pelvic Inflammatory Disease), a major cause of sterility, in women. PID Symptoms: fever, pain during sex, abdominal pain. Can cause arthritis.

Transmission: Close sexual contact or can be carried on hands to eyes.

Symptoms: Mild symptoms at first. Many women and some men have none. When present in men: painful urination, watery discharge from penis. In women: itching, burning in genitals, vaginal discharge, dull pelvic pain, bleeding between menstrual periods. Medical diagnosis needed.

Potential Effects: Very serious even with mild or no symptoms. Untreated, causes sterility. In men, can lead to arthritis and inflammation of testicles. In women, infection of cervix (lower part of uterus) can spread, causing scar tissue in tubes and painful PID (pelvic inflammatory disease). If passed to infant during birth process, causes eye infections, pneumonia.

Occurrence: Fastest spreading STD in U.S., especially among 15 to 25-year-olds. Four million people are infected each year; 100,000 become sterile. Men with Chlamydia must tell their partners immediately because women sometimes don't have symptoms.

Treatment: Medical diagnosis under microscope from tissue sample or blood test. Can be cured with antibiotics. Gonorrhea often hides Chlamydia. Treatment for Gonorrhea won't cure Chlamydia. Sexually active people should have a test once a year for Chlamydia. Treatment has 95% cure rate.

GENITAL WARTS (ALSO KNOWN AS HUMAN PAPILLOMA VIRUS-HPV)

What is it? Viral infection (HPV) leads to growths (Genital Warts) that appear on penis, vulva, vagina, cervix, in or around anus or in throat. Increasing, especially among teenagers, who are at high risk. Warts may be tiny or like cauliflowers, or flat. Must be treated immediately.

Transmission: Virus is spread by genital or oral sex contact with someone who has the HPV virus, or from touching skin to skin. Wart may appear a few weeks after contact or months later. Can harbor virus for many years without any signs of infection. When exposed, 60-70% will get it.

Symptoms: There may be no symptoms. It's called the "silent" epidemic. Or, 1 to 3 months after contact cauliflower-like bumps appear inside and outside genitals and/or rectum. May cause irritation or itch. Often painless. Bumps may be very tiny, hard to see, but they spread fast.

Potential Effects: Very dangerous. Extra risk of cancer of cervix, vulva, penis or anus among people who have or have had HPV infection, even if warts are gone. Several different strains of HPV cause at least 90% of all cervical cancer.[39] Babies born to women with HPV can get warts in their throats. NO CURE. Virus remains even after warts are gone; still infectious.

Occurrence: Very common and spreading rapidly, especially among teenagers who are at very high risk because their skin is still maturing. New test accurately determines when a woman has been infected, used with Pap smear, detects cervical cancer early. Once you test positive, doctor must monitor you closely. Three million affected each year.

Treatment: Warts are treated with a very toxic ointment, frozen off or burned off with laser or electric needle, under anesthetic. Not fun! Pregnant women require special treatment. For mild infection, doctor applies special ointment to warts during several weekly visits. If warts come back treatment must be repeated. NO CURE.

GONORRHEA (ALSO KNOWN AS CLAP, DOSE, DRIP)

What is it? Infection caused by gonococcus bacteria that can live only in dark, warm, moist places, like inside your body — cervix, penis, throat or rectum. Can cause PID (Pelvic Inflammatory Disease) which, untreated, may cause sterility.

Transmission: Most always through sexual intercourse. In sexual foreplay, if genitals touch, even without intercourse, infection can occur.

Symptoms: Nothing for 2-9 days, then frequent painful burning urination and whitish, greenish or yellow discharge from penis or vagina. In men, opening of penis may be red and sore. Other symptoms: sore throat, swollen glands, discharge from anus. Sometimes there are no symptoms. Diagnosis by examining culture.

Potential Effects: Won't go away by itself even if symptoms disappear. Women may get PID; men, chronic painful urination and ejaculation. Can cause sterility and arthritis in both sexes, and blindness if eyes are infected. Pregnant women can infect their unborn babies.

Occurrence: A million cases reported each year. That's only half the actual number. Most occur in people between ages of 18-25. New strain of penicillin-resistant Gonorrhea (PPNG) is sweeping the country. About 1 per 100, 15 to 19-year-olds have Gonorrhea.

Treatment: Doctor will prescribe proper antibiotic. Take all the prescribed dose. Chlamydia is often present with Gonorrhea, so both conditions should be treated at same time. No sex until there are two negative cultures. Both partners should be treated to avoid reinfection.

HEPATITIS

What is it? Four different types of Hepatitis (Type A, Type B, Type Non-A Non-B, Type C) caused by different viruses can be transmitted in several different ways. Type B (sexually transmitted) is most dangerous with symptoms much like AIDS but usually not fatal. Hepatitis C is similar but is not as commonly passed sexually as B.

Transmission: Type A: Spread by sexual contact with infected person or by sex acts such as oral/anal or finger/anal sex play. Also spread by person who has it and doesn't wash hands after using toilet. Virus gets on things he or she touches, like food. Type B (serum hepatitis) spread by mouth/mouth, mouth/genital or other sex contact or unclean surgical needles. Non-A Non-B: by blood transfusion or sexual contact.

Symptoms: Appear within month after contact. In some cases: muscle ache, fever, tiredness, loss of appetite, headaches, dizziness (like flu symptoms). In other cases: dark urine, light stool color, yellow eyes and skin (jaundice), tenderness in liver area.

Potential Effects: Highly infectious in early stages. Makes a person very sick because it affects liver and all body functions. Baby born to woman with Type B may develop it and become chronic carrier. Untreated, may develop into chronic liver disease. Type B can lead to fatal disease.

Occurrence: Very common.

Treatment: Doctor must diagnose. Get bed rest, even in hospital, until severe symptoms disappear (about 2 weeks). May take weeks or months to recover fully. No liquor during convalescence. Use a birth control method other than the pill until completely cured. Safe, effective vaccine is available for Hepatitis B.

HERPES SIMPLEX VIRUS-II (ALSO KNOWN AS GENITAL HERPES)

What is it? Painful, blister-like sores that appear on and in penis, vagina and/or anus; sometimes around mouth. There is NO CURE, only medical relief. Herpes goes away but may return. Average patient has 4 to 7 flare-ups a year. They become less frequent with time.

Transmission: By sexual contact. Highly contagious if there are open sores but can be spread even after sores heal. Virus from one person's sores enters the other's body through cuts, genital openings, mouth. Moves from one part of body to another when you touch infected area.

Symptoms: About 2-20 days after contact, painful blisters appear on penis or in vagina and/or cervix, pubic area, thighs, buttocks. May include swollen lymph glands, aching muscles, fever, headaches. Blisters dry up and go away, leaving painful sores. Blisters return when victim is under stress. Recurring attacks less painful, heal faster.

Potential Effects: Highly infectious. Sores are painful. Herpes-II virus remains in body. There is a link between Herpes-II and cervical cancer, so women with Herpes must have Pap smear twice yearly. Can cause Herpes Encephalitis and/or blindness in newborns. Cesarean section recommended for women with active Herpes.

Occurrence: VERY common. 500,000 to 1 million new cases each year. Pregnant women with Herpes II can infect babies; 3,000 to 10,000 newborns infected yearly. Average male has 40-50% chance of being infected with Herpes (HSV II) and may unknowingly pass along the infection.

Treatment: No cure. Treatment—Acyclovir (antiviral prescription ointment or capsule) eases pain, shortens attack. Herpes may seem to go away after treatment. That doesn't mean it's gone! Too much sun seems to cause attacks. Avoid sex, tight clothes during attack.

PUBIC LICE (ALSO KNOWN AS CRABS)

What is it? Parasites (tiny bugs) that live in hair around penis or vagina.

Transmission: Usually sexual contact but also by infected towels, toilet seats, bedding, clothing.

Symptoms: Severe itching, sometimes blood on underwear from places lice have gotten under skin. Sometimes lice can be seen in the hairy parts of your body.

Potential Effects: Not dangerous, but highly contagious. Crabs can move from pubic hair to other hairy places in body (under arms, eyelashes) as you scratch, then touch other places.

Occurrence: Common if good hygiene is not practiced. Bathe or shower daily.

Treatment: Kwell (by prescription) or nonprescription RID or R & C as cream, lotion or shampoo works fast and well. Repeat treatment in one week. No sex during treatment. Both partners must be treated. Keep clean. Wash all clothes, bedding in HOT water.

SCABIES

What is it? Infestation of tiny mites (bugs) that burrow under skin.

Transmission: Sexual contact or other close physical contact. Can travel person to person by kissing, hugging, and from dirty toilets.

Symptoms: Reddish zigzag furrows under skin, usually in genital area and buttocks, but also between fingers, skin folds of elbows, wrists, under arms, breasts, feet. Painful itching.

Potential Effects: Scabies often spreads through a family.

Occurrence: Where people live in crowded conditions and do not bathe.

Treatment: See doctor or clinic. Treatment—Cream obtained by prescription applied from neck down and left on for prescribed period before washing it off.

SYPHILIS (ALSO KNOWN AS SYPH, POX, BAD BLOOD)

What is it? Small spiral shaped bacteria called "spirochetes" that enter body, usually by sexual contact. Once in body, they enter bloodstream, infect vital organs.

Transmission: Sexual contact. Sores around mouth or genitals of infected person (or anywhere spirochetes can hide) pass bacteria to sex partner. Can be transmitted from infected person to open cut in skin of another person.

Symptoms: First stage: 10-90 days after exposure, a hard red, usually painless raised spot appears at site of infection (usually penis or vulva but can be on lips, mouth or anus). Goes away in week or two. 2nd stage (weeks or months later): Rash may cover body or just palms of hands, soles of feet. Sore throat, fever, itch. Can attack almost any body part. Hair may fall out. Get help immediately! Symptoms may disappear without treatment but will return in 5, 10 or 20 years for final stage which may be fatal.

Potential Effects: Untreated syphilis doesn't go away but hides in blood, lymph glands. Sometimes 1st stage has no symptoms, or sore is so small you think it's a pimple. Any sore around mouth or genitals must be treated seriously. 1st and 2nd stage symptoms may vanish but 3rd stage causes invalidism, blindness, senility, death.

Occurrence: Dramatic increase in number of Syphilis cases, especially among teenagers. Also an increase in congenital Syphilis in which an infected mother passes the disease to her unborn child.

Treatment: Special tests available in Public Health clinics detect Syphilis in stages 1, 2 or 3. Treatment—

Large doses of penicillin or other antibiotic for as long as needed until cured. Sexual activity is prohibited until cured; blood tests are required every 3 months for 2 years to confirm cure. If not treated correctly, Syphilis can erupt years later as 3rd stage Syphilis with serious consequences.

TRICHOMONIASIS (ALSO KNOWN AS TRICH)

What is it? Infection of vagina in women, urethra in men, caused by tiny parasites that live in moist places in the body.

Transmission: Sexual contact. Also spread by damp washcloths, towels and bathing suits shared with infected person. Parasite can live outside body for 7 hours.

Symptoms: In women, greenish yellow vaginal discharge with bad odor, frequent painful urination, inflammation in genitals, sometimes pain in lower abdomen. In men, discharge from penis, mild discomfort in penis. You can harbor Trich in your body for years with or without symptoms.

Potential Effects: Drug prescribed for treatment (Flagyl) may cause dizziness, nausea and headache. Pregnant women should not use Flagyl.

Occurrence: Common but minor. Prompt treatment cures.

Treatment: Best treatment is prevention. Flagyl (by prescription) is treatment for this and many parasitic organisms. Both partners should be treated to prevent reinfection.

[1] Scripture quotations from *The MESSAGE*. Copyright © by Eugene H. Peterson 1993, 1994, 1995. Used by permission of NAVPRESS Publishing Group.

[2] McDowell and Day. *Why Wait.* Thomas Nelson Publishers, Nashville, TN, 1987, p. 56.

[3] Ibid. *The MESSAGE.*

[4] The Alan Guttmacher Institute. *Sex and America's Teenagers.* New York: Author, 1994, p. 45.

[5] Ibid.

[6] The Medical Institute for Sexual Health. P.O. Box 4919, Austin, TX 78765, 1996.

[7] U.S. Dept. of Health & Human Services, Public Health Service. Centers for Disease Control, 1991 *Division of STD/HIV Prevention.* Annual Report. p. 13.

[8] Institute of Medicine, 1996.

[9] HIV/AIDS Surveillance Report. Vol. 8, (1). Centers for Disease Control, U.S. Department of Health & Human Services, June 1996.

[10] Weller, S.C. A meta-analysis of condom effectiveness in reducing sexually transmitted HIV. *Social Science Medicine.* Vol. 36, (12), 1993, pp. 1635-1644.

[11] Kay tone. Sexually Transmitted Diseases Division, Centers for Disease Control, U.S. Dept. of Health & Human Services. t.i., March l6, 1992.

[12] The Medical Institute for Sexual Health. P.O. Box 4919, Austin, TX 78765, 1996.

[13] Jones, E.F., & F.D. Forrest. Contraceptive failure in the United States: Revised estimates from the 1982 National Survey of Family Growth. *Family Planning Perspectives,* Vol. 21 (3), 1989, pp. 103-109.

[14] Cates, W., & K.M Stone. Committee on Adolescence. Condom availability for adolescents. *American College of Obstetrics and Gynecology, (*154), 1995.
Hatcher, R.A. et al. *Contraceptive Technology* (16th edition). New York: Irvington. 1994, pp. 157, 641-642.
Trussell, J., D. Warner, & R. Hatcher. Condom performance during vaginal intercourse; Comparison of Trojan-Eng and Tactylon condoms. *Contraception,* Vol. 45 (1), 1992, pp. 11-19.

[15] Center for Devices and Radiological Health. Department of Health & Human Services, Food and Drug Administration.

[16] Ibid. Cates, W. & K.M. Stone.

[17] The Medical Institute for Sexual Health. P.O. Box 4919, Austin, TX 78765, 1996.
[18] Ibid.
[19] Vincent M. Rue. "The Psychological Realities of Induced Abortion," *Post-Abortion Aftermath: A Comprehensive Consideration,* Michael T. Mannion, Editor, Sheed & Ward. 1994, pp. 5-43.
[20] Bethany Christian Services. *A Loving Choice.* 901 Eastern Ave. N.E., Grand Rapids, MI 49503, 1988, p.7.
[21] The U.S. Department of Commerce. Bureau of Census, *Current Population Reports,* Series P-20, (445), Washington, D.C.: U.S. Government Printing Office, 1990.
[22] Ibid. *A Loving Choice.*
[23] Institute of Medicine, 1997.
[24] Centers for Disease Control, 1990.
[25] The Alan Guttmacher Institute. *Sex and America's Teenagers,* New York: Author, 1994, p. 30.
Institute of Medicine, 1996. Eng, T., & W.T. Butler, 1996. *The Hidden Epidemic: Confronting Sexually Transmitted Diseases.* Washington, DC: National Academy Press, pp. 2-5.
[26] Ibid, Cates, W., & K.M. Stone.
Jamison, J.H. et al. Spectrum of genital human papilloma virus infection in a female adolescent population. *Sexually Transmitted Diseases,* Vol. 21 (3), 1995, pp. 236-243.
[27] Center for Devices and Radiological Health, Department of Health & Human Services, Food and Drug Administration, 1994.
[28] Centers For Disease Control and Prevention. Update: Barrier protection against HIV infection and other sexually transmitted diseases. *Morbidity and Mortality Weekly Report,* Vol. 37, 1988, pp. 133-137.
[29] Ibid, Weller, S.C. 1993.
[30] This material is taken from *My Utmost for His Highest* by Oswald Chambers, edited by James Reimann, © 1992 by Oswald Chambers Publications Assn., Ltd. Original edition © 1935 by Dodd Mead & Co., renewed 1963 by the Oswald Chambers Publications Assn., Ltd., and is used by permission of Discovery House Publishers, Box 3566, Grand Rapids MI 49501. All rights reserved.
[31] *U.S. News & World Report.* April 15, 1996, Vol. 120 (15), p.58.
[32] *USA Today.* Nov. 1996, Vol.125 (2618), p.60.

[33] Ibid. *The MESSAGE.*

[34] The Advocate Survey. August 23, 1994.

[35] *The Wounded Heart,* Dr. Dan B. Allender, © 1990, used by permission of NAVPRESS/PINON PRESS. All rights reserved. For Copies call 1-800-366-7788.

[36] The Alan Guttmacher Institute. *Sex and America's Teenagers,* New York: Author, 1994, p.45.

[37] Pipher, Mary Ph.D. (1994). *Reviving Ophelia, Saving the Selves of Adolescent Girls,* Ballantine Books, New York.

[38] *"Most sexually active teens don't use condoms"*, The Atlanta Journal and Constitution, Jan. 4, 1992.

[39] National Institutes of Health. *Consensus Development Conference Statement on Cervical Cancer.* Kensington, MD:NIH Consensus Program Information Service , Eng, T., & W.T. Butler (eds.) *The Hidden Epidemic: Confronting Sexually Transmitted Diseases.* Washington, DC: National Academy Press, 1996, pp. 2-5.

DEMONSTRATIONS

LET'S THINK ABOUT IT...

WORKSHEETS/ HANDOUTS

ABOUT THE AUTHOR:

Gayle Bucher, a wife and mother of two daughters, is also an educator, speaker and counselor to teenagers and women. She is the author of CREATING POSITIVE RELATIONSHIPS, a sexual abstinence program designed for public schools and CREATING POSITIVE RELATIONSHIPS **PLUS**, designed for parochial schools and church youth groups.

Her passion for helping teenagers with sexual issues came as a result of one of the most painful times in her life. Struggling with infertility, she and her husband pursued adoption. In gratitude to their daughter's birth mother, she felt compelled to help young people avoid the agonizing choices of an unplanned pregnancy. Her work at a crisis pregnancy center convinced her of the need for abstinence-based sexual education and supportive education for parents to better communicate their sexual values to their children.